BEST CLINICAL PRACTICES FOR

TREATING FAMILIES IN JUVENILE AND CRIMINAL JUSTICE SYSTEMS

Fundamentals of Clinical Practice With Couples and Families Series

Best Clinical Practices for Treating Families in Juvenile and Criminal Justice Systems
Corinne C. Datchi

BEST CLINICAL PRACTICES FOR

TREATING FAMILIES IN JUVENILE AND CRIMINAL JUSTICE SYSTEMS

CORINNE C. DATCHI

AMERICAN PSYCHOLOGICAL ASSOCIATION

Published by
American Psychological Association
750 First Street, NE
Washington, DC 20002
https://www.apa.org

Order Department
https://www.apa.org/pubs/books
order@apa.org

In the U.K., Europe, Africa, and the Middle East, copies may be ordered from Eurospan
https://www.eurospanbookstore.com/apa
info@eurospangroup.com

Typeset in Charter and Interstate by Circle Graphics, Inc., Reisterstown, MD

Printer: Gasch Printing, Odenton, MD
Cover Designer: Mark Karis

Library of Congress Cataloging-in-Publication Data

Names: Datchi, Corinne C., author.
Title: Best clinical practices for treating families in juvenile and criminal justice systems / by Corinne C. Datchi.
Description: Washington, DC : American Psychological Association, [2022] | Series: Fundamentals of clinical practice with couples and families | Includes bibliographical references and index.
Identifiers: LCCN 2021040172 (print) | LCCN 2021040173 (ebook) | ISBN 9781433836558 (paperback) | ISBN 9781433839269 (ebook)
Subjects: LCSH: Criminals--Rehabilitation--United States. | Juvenile delinquents--Rehabilitation--United States. | Prisoners' families--United States. | Family psychotherapy--United States.
Classification: LCC HV9304 .D37 2022 (print) | LCC HV9304 (ebook) | DDC 364.360973--dc23
LC record available at https://lccn.loc.gov/2021040172
LC ebook record available at https://lccn.loc.gov/2021040173

https://doi.org/10.1037/0000285-000

Printed in the United States of America

10 9 8 7 6 5 4 3 2 1

Contents

Series Preface

CORINNE C. DATCHI AND ANTHONY L. CHAMBERS

Couple and family therapy represents a major area of clinical practice in the mental health professions. In 2012, an estimated 75% of practicing psychologists worked with couples in a conjoint format, and 33% provided family services (Norcross & Rogan, 2013). Future projections suggest that the field of couple and family therapy will grow 22% between 2019 and 2029 (U.S. Bureau of Labor Statistics, 2021). These are relatively high rates that reflect the increased understanding of the link between individual mental health and couple and family relationships. They also suggest a growing emphasis on integrative and ecological treatment approaches that target the person and their immediate environment.

We, the editors of this book series, are board-certified couple and family psychologists involved in research and clinical activities with diverse individuals, couples, and families. We have at least 15 years of experience in the specialty of couple and family psychology, as practitioners, scholars, and educators. We have trained and supervised graduate students and clinicians to work with couples and families in various settings, including university clinics, community-based mental health agencies, and criminal justice systems. Couple and family psychology is a core dimension of our professional identity, and systems thinking is the primary conceptual lens that guides our professional activities.

We have created this book series to support competency-based education and training for specialty practice with couples and families at the graduate, postgraduate, and postlicensure levels. Our goal is to highlight the distinctive knowledge and skills that are required to work effectively with diverse couples and families. We seek to showcase best practices in the treatment of couples and families, based on the most current research in psychology and psychotherapy.

The series consists of short books that discuss specialty assessment, case conceptualization, intervention, and consultation for clinical practice with couples and families. The books are written by field experts and designed to be clinical guides. They provide comprehensive summaries of the specialty knowledge needed to work with specific clinical populations and mental health concerns. They also demonstrate how to use the specialty skills to treat specific populations of couples and families in various settings.

The focus on using a systemic theoretical framework is a common thread that links the books together. The key concepts and principles of systems theory are used to organize knowledge about couples and families and to discuss treatment decisions. Systemic thinking emphasizes a holistic approach to clinical practice. It calls for the ability to see the person in interaction with their context and to observe how the dynamic factors in and around the person influence each other, the progression of clinical problems, and the course of treatment.

The focus on specialty competencies is also a common thread that links the books together. These are the specialty competencies for professional practice with couples and families endorsed by the American Board of Couple and Family Psychology (2020). The Board has recognized 16 competencies that represent the systemic knowledge, skills, values, and attitudes of couple and family psychology. A detailed discussion of each of the competencies, their components, and behavioral anchors can be found in Mark Stanton and Robert Welsh's seminal book, *Specialty Competencies in Couple and Family Psychology*, published by Oxford University Press in 2011.

Professional competence is both an outcome of education and training and an ethical imperative to protect the welfare of the public (Stanton & Harway, 2019). The term refers to clinicians' overall suitability for the delivery of mental health services (Rubin et al., 2007). Competence is context specific: Different clinical settings and populations require different kinds of expertise (Falender & Shafranske, 2017). Developing competence is a dynamic and ongoing process of learning rather than an endpoint.

Competencies are interrelated sets of knowledge, skills, attitudes, and values that are observable and measurable (Rubin et al., 2007). They are grouped into two categories: (a) foundational and (b) functional. *Foundational competencies* (e.g., the capacity to engage in self-reflective practice, knowledge, and application of ethical standards) are a prerequisite for the development of *functional competencies* (knowledge and skills used to work with clients); they are the basis for all professional activities, including assessment, diagnosis, conceptualization, intervention, consultation, research and evaluation, supervision and teaching, and administration and management (Rubin et al., 2007).

Competencies for clinical practice with couples and families require specialty education and training at the doctoral, postdoctoral, and/or postlicensure stage. The Couple and Family Psychology Specialty Council, which represents three organizations (American Board of Couple and Family Psychology; American Academy of Couple and Family Psychology; and American Psychological Association Division 43, the Society for Couple and Family Psychology), has recently adopted education and training guidelines for model doctoral, internship, postdoctoral, and postlicensure programs in couple and family psychology (Riggs et al., 2020). These guidelines follow the taxonomy developed by the Council of Specialties in Professional Psychology (2021) and specify the didactic and experiential components necessary for developing different levels of competence in clinical practice with couples and families.

The majority of doctoral psychology programs in the United States provide some exposure to couple and family psychology, most often through a survey course that focuses on it (Regas & Becerra, 2013). However, exposure is not sufficient to develop competence in the specialty. The American Board of Couple and Family Psychology (2016) recommends additional postgraduation experiences to demonstrate appropriate specialty education and training, for example: a predoctoral internship with a track in couple and family psychology; a postdoctoral fellowship with 30% to 50% of supervised practice with couples and families; at least 25 hours of postlicensure continuing education, specific to couple and family psychology; and at least 25 hours of specialty supervision by a board certified couple and family psychologist.

This book series is intended to expand access to specialty education in clinical practice with couples and families. It is designed for a diverse audience of mental health practitioners with different levels of training and experience. Graduate students and postdoctoral Fellows will find it useful to increase their understanding of systemic thinking, assessment, case conceptualization, and intervention with couples and families and to support their application of systemic principles in the treatment of clinical problems. Seasoned clinicians—psychologists, social workers, counselors, and marriage and family therapists—will also find the series useful to keep current with new practice developments and to build on their specialty knowledge and skills.

Best Clinical Practices for Treating Families in Juvenile and Criminal Justice Systems is one of the first published books in the series. As the title suggests, it focuses on the treatment issues of justice-involved populations and their families and examines how interactions among multiple systems—the person, the family, corrections, and the mental health system—influence the psychosocial outcomes of at-risk individuals with a criminal history. It demonstrates why it is critical to support and engage partners, spouses, and other family members in the treatment of juvenile and adult offenders. It also describes how to provide evidence-based services that focus on couple and family resilience and enhance the effectiveness of offender rehabilitation in correctional and community settings. This book discusses the distinctive knowledge and skills that are required for specialty competence with justice-involved couples and families. It also defines the conceptual elements of a systemic framework for working with forensic populations in the juvenile and criminal justice systems.

REFERENCES

American Board of Couple and Family Psychology. (2016, September). *Manual for obtaining board certification*. https://www.abpp.org/BlankSite/media/Couple-and-Family-Psychology-Documents/ABCFP-Manual.pdf

American Board of Couple and Family Psychology. (2020, June 1). *Couple & family psychology*. https://abpp.org/Applicant-Information/Specialty-Boards/Couple-and-Family-Psychology.aspx

Council of Specialties in Professional Psychology. (2021). *2021 CoS taxonomy initiative*. https://www.cospp.org/2021-cos-taxonomy-initiative

Falender, C. A., & Shafranske, E. P. (2017). *Supervision essentials for the practice of competency-based supervision*. American Psychological Association.

Norcross, J. C., & Rogan, J. D. (2013). Psychologists conducting psychotherapy in 2012: Current practices and historical trends among Division 29 members. *Psychotherapy*, *50*(4), 490–495. https://doi.org/10.1037/a0033512

Regas, S., & Becerra, A. (2013). *Division 43 survey: Educating and training psychologists: Report to the Division 43 board*. American Psychological Association.

Riggs, S., Sanchez, J., Pollard, S., Sanford, G., & Wise, C. (2020). *Couple and family psychology training and education guidelines: Report to the Division 43 board*. American Psychological Association.

Rubin, N. J., Bebeau, M., Leigh, I. W., Lichtenberg, J. W., Nelson, P. D., Portnoy, S., Smith, I. L., & Kaslow, N. J. (2007). The competency movement within psychology: An historical perspective. *Professional Psychology: Research and Practice*, *38*(5), 452–462. https://doi.org/10.1037/0735-7028.38.5.452

Stanton, M., & Harway, M. (2019). Graduate education in couple and family psychology. In B. H. Fiese (Ed.), *APA handbook of contemporary family psychology* (Vol. 3, pp. 469–482). American Psychological Association.

Stanton, M., & Welsh, R. (2011). *Specialty competencies in couple and family psychology*. Oxford University Press. https://doi.org/10.1093/med:psych/9780195387872.001.0001

U.S. Bureau of Labor Statistics. (2021, April 9). *Occupational outlook handbook: Marriage and family therapists*. https://www.bls.gov/ooh/community-and-social-service/marriage-and-family-therapists.htm

BEST CLINICAL PRACTICES FOR

TREATING FAMILIES IN JUVENILE AND CRIMINAL JUSTICE SYSTEMS

INTRODUCTION

Treating Families in Juvenile and Criminal Justice Systems

The intersection between mental health and justice has expanded in the recent past. Individuals with severe mental disorders come into contact with the police and the courts at rates higher than the general population (Ghiasi et al., 2021; Office of Juvenile Justice and Delinquency Prevention, 2017a). Most have limited access to psychiatric services in the community. Prisons and jails are often the only places where they can find medical and mental health care (Cloud et al., 2014; Lilliott et al., 2017).

The crossing of mental health and justice has led to new developments in legal and therapeutic programming. For example, mental health and drug treatment courts represent current efforts in the juvenile and criminal justice systems to form partnerships with mental health providers and address the psychiatric needs of justice-involved populations (Datchi, 2017b). To be effective, interprofessional partnerships require that mental health and justice practitioners coordinate treatment and legal interventions based on a shared understanding of their respective roles, activities, and responsibilities.

This book centers on a specific area of mental health practice that intersects with the legal system: couple and family services for justice-involved

https://doi.org/10.1037/0000285-001
Best Clinical Practices for Treating Families in Juvenile and Criminal Justice Systems, by C. C. Datchi

populations that include couple and family treatment programs and psychoeducation. A substantive number of publications discuss evidence-based couple and family therapy models for juvenile delinquency. They offer excellent guides for model-specific case conceptualization, treatment planning, and interventions (e.g., Alexander et al., 2013; Sexton, 2011; Szapocznik et al., 2003). By contrast, this book describes a competency-based approach to clinical practice with justice-involved couples and families.

COMPETENCY-BASED CLINICAL PRACTICE

The concept of *professional competence* describes the qualifications a clinician must possess in order to work effectively and provide quality mental health services (J. K. Miller et al., 2010; Stanton & Welsh, 2011). It involves a set of competencies—knowledge, skills, attitudes, and values—that fall into two domains: foundational and functional (Rubin et al., 2007). *Foundational competencies* are the knowledge, skills, attitudes, and values that form the basis for effective clinical activities. They are categorized as follows: reflective practices and self-assessment, scientific knowledge and methods, relationships and interpersonal interactions, ethical and legal standards, policy and advocacy issues, individual and cultural diversity, and interdisciplinary systems (Rubin et al., 2007). *Functional competencies* relate to various dimensions of clinical practice: assessment, diagnosis, and case conceptualization; intervention; consultation; research and evaluation; supervision; and management and administration.

This book focuses on the functional competencies of assessment, case conceptualization, and intervention necessary to work effectively with couples and families in the juvenile and criminal justice systems. These competencies include skills and strategies that are required for effective practice with couples and families as well as knowledge of the juvenile and criminal justice systems and familiarity with family systems theory and forensic mental health issues (Stanton & Welsh, 2011). With regard to knowledge about justice-involved populations, this book describes the salient characteristics of youth and adults who come into contact with law enforcement and the courts. This information is important to the recognition of the psychological, social, and diversity factors that account for individuals' entanglement with justice and that have an impact on couple and family functioning. An understanding of these factors is incorporated into the systemic assessment, conceptualization, and treatment of clinical problems in the context of couple and family relationships.

MORE ABOUT THE BOOK

This book is part of a series that illustrates the application of specialty professional competencies in the treatment of couples and families with diverse concerns. It focuses on the relational and mental health needs of couples and families who are involved directly and indirectly with the U.S. juvenile and criminal justice systems. It does not examine family issues (e.g., divorce, child custody evaluations) that occur in other legal arenas (e.g., family courts). It is not a book about actuarial risk assessment and correctional treatment. It aims instead to demonstrate the value of a family-oriented approach to rehabilitative programming. “Offender rehabilitation” is a term commonly used to define a range of services that address the risk factors associated with recidivism (National Institute of Justice, 2020): group work, counseling, mentoring, cognitive behavioral programs, vocational training, substance abuse treatment, and so on. This book shows that couple and family interventions are critical components of offender rehabilitation for both youth and adults; couple and family services can support positive family involvement and enhance justice solutions to delinquency and crime.

This book is written for clinicians who work or will work with forensic populations in mental health agencies and correctional facilities, mostly youth and adults referred by juvenile and criminal courts and serving a sentence in the community or behind bars. The intended audience includes social workers, professional counselors, family therapists, psychologists, and graduate trainees who have varied levels of familiarity with the justice system. This book is designed to increase readers’ knowledge of the couple and family processes that influence change in criminal conduct and to develop their skills and ability to make effective decisions about the assessment and treatment of justice-involved individuals and their relationships.

ORGANIZATION OF THE BOOK

This book is organized into six chapters that build on each other. The chapters present foundational knowledge for clinical practice with justice-involved couples and families, with a focus on systems thinking and scientific knowledge about couple and family dynamics and therapy programs. They also describe the application of functional competencies in couple and family psychology that are relevant to assessment, case conceptualization, and intervention. In this book, the term *family* designates individuals’ extended network of interpersonal bonds based on blood or other intimate ties, marriage, and adoption; this includes the nuclear family and less immediate relatives. The term *offender* is used in discussions that examine theoretical and scientific knowledge about criminal conduct; it refers to individuals who have committed acts prohibited under the law and who are now the target of intervention by justice professionals. The concept of *criminal conduct* refers to the lawbreaking behaviors that are the focus of the criminal and juvenile justice systems.

To show the application of foundational and functional competencies with justice-involved couples and families, this book follows a case study approach: Chapters 2 through 5 provide an in-depth examination of a fictitious family: Sam, Sara, Gabriel, and Julia. This family illustrates the concerns and difficulties of many individuals and their relatives in the juvenile and criminal justice systems.

Chapter 1 sets the stage for the discussion that follows. It describes the context in which treatment occurs and explains how youth and adults come into contact with and are handled by the juvenile and criminal justice systems. It reviews the psychological theories that inform correctional programming and proposes a family systems approach to offender rehabilitation that incorporates the key concepts and principles of systemic thinking.

Chapter 2 tells the story of Sam, Sara, Gabriel, and Julia's involvement with law enforcement, the courts, and corrections. Their story highlights the individual and cultural diversity factors that define the experience of youth, adults, couples, and families in the juvenile and criminal justice systems. Information about race–ethnicity, gender, educational attainment, employment, and mental health helps to discern the contextual factors (e.g., family violence, racial disparities) that influence the odds of justice involvement. In particular, Chapter 2 calls attention to the prevalence of traumatic stress, severe mental illness, and addiction among justice-involved populations who report superior rates of victimization and psychiatric and substance use disorders compared with the general public. These statistics highlight the psychosocial needs of juvenile and adult offenders in the U.S. justice system. This knowledge is incorporated into the contextual assessment and case conceptualization of the fictitious family in Chapter 4.

Chapter 3 discusses recent empirical findings on the predictors of delinquency and crime. It starts with a review of the concepts of risk and protective factors in the criminology and psychology literature. These factors exist at different levels of the person's ecology: intrapersonal, relational, and environmental. Their reciprocal interactions influence the likelihood that an individual will engage in criminal behaviors and acts of violence. In particular, Chapter 3 highlights the role of family processes in mediating the effects of individual and contextual factors on juvenile and adult recidivism. It also includes a discussion of the impact of justice involvement on family dynamics. This knowledge is essential to clinical practice with couples and families: Relational processes are the primary focus of couple- and family-based therapy programs; the risk and protective factors that predict offending constitute sites of intervention. Chapter 3 shows how to apply evidence-based knowledge about the predictors of antisocial behavior to understand the challenges of the fictitious family.

Chapter 4 reviews the components of systemic assessment and case conceptualization and describes how to create a therapeutic frame with justice-involved couples and families. The discussion is focused on family engagement, the therapeutic alliance, the sources of information, and the selection of methods to gather data about the family and the problem. Chapter 4 shows how to conduct a systemic assessment, how to interpret qualitative and quantitative data, and how to organize the case conceptualization using the example of the fictitious family. It also demonstrates how to navigate the unique challenges of clinical practice with justice-involved couples and families.

Chapter 5 presents the current state of the evidence on couple and family therapy with justice-involved populations and includes available information about the cost-effectiveness of family interventions for juvenile offenders. It provides detailed summaries of well-established family therapy programs that have been shown to reduce delinquency and improve family functioning. Each summary answers questions about patient demographics, delivery format, treatment goals, therapeutic processes, and outcomes. Chapter 5 also describes the adaptation of evidence-based family interventions and marriage education programs for adult offenders. It is intended to advance the reader's knowledge of evidence-based practices in clinical practice with justice-involved couples and families, which is a benchmark of professional competence.

Chapter 6 demonstrates how to use evidence-based knowledge about effective therapeutic models in the treatment of justice-involved families; specifically, it shows how clinicians formulate a treatment plan and select interventions on the basis of the results of their assessment and case conceptualization. It also describes treatment monitoring and interprofessional collaboration as critical aspects of clinical practice with couples and families and discusses common treatment challenges with justice-involved families. The case of Sam, Sara, Gabriel, and Julia serves to illustrate each activity, from treatment planning to treatment coordination.

1 PSYCHOLOGY AND JUSTICE

A Family Systems Approach to Offender Rehabilitation

Whatever affects one directly, affects all indirectly. I can never be what I ought to be until you are what you ought to be. This is the interrelated structure of reality.

—Martin Luther King, Jr., Commencement Address,
Oberlin College, 1965

Since the 1980s, the criminal justice population in the United States has grown from approximately 2 million to 7 million individuals (The Sentencing Project, 2021). It is estimated that one in 38 adults age 18 and over are under some form of correctional supervision (Kaeble & Cowhig, 2018). Those include individuals who are confined in jail or prison (three in 10 individuals under correctional supervision in 2017; Bronson & Carson, 2019; Zeng, 2019) and offenders on probation or parole in the community (seven in 10 in 2017; Jones, 2018; Kaeble, 2018; Kaeble & Cowhig, 2018). Another 10 million people were arrested in 2018 (Federal Bureau of Investigation, 2019). Likewise, there were about 820,000 delinquency cases in 2017 (Office of Juvenile

https://doi.org/10.1037/0000285-002
Best Clinical Practices for Treating Families in Juvenile and Criminal Justice Systems, by C. C. Datchi

Justice and Delinquency Prevention [OJJDP], n.d.-a, n.d.-b). Less than half (43%) were either dismissed or handled informally. The majority (57%) of delinquent cases were referred to juvenile courts for formal processing, and 53% of those referrals were adjudicated or declared by a judge to be delinquent (OJJDP, 2019). Of adjudicated cases, 28% were sent to a residential facility and 63% were placed on formal probation.

These statistics highlight the prominence of the juvenile and criminal justice systems in U.S. society. They also indicate their far-reaching impact on families, close and extended relatives, friends, and neighbors who become involved with the justice system through their relationships with offenders. It is estimated that one in 14 children have experienced parental incarceration in their youth (The Annie E. Casey Foundation, 2016), and one in 28 children have a father and/or mother currently in jail or prison (The Pew Charitable Trusts, 2010). A 2017 survey of the U.S. population showed that 64% of Americans had a close or distant relative behind bars for one night or longer during their lifetime (Enns et al., 2019). Sibling incarceration was the most prevalent type of family contact with the correctional system. Black families (61%–63%) and individuals with low levels of education (60%) were more likely to have experienced the incarceration of a family member. Family research has also highlighted the effects of parental incarceration on family stability and children's outcomes in the United States (Martin, 2017). Less attention has been given to family involvement in other arenas of the criminal justice system, such as problem-solving courts, prisoner reentry, and adult parole or probation.

It is difficult to determine the neighborhood-level effects of criminal justice involvement (National Research Council, 2014); however, research has shown that incarceration and other contact with legal institutions (e.g., police, courts) occur at higher rates and more frequently in poor, urban, Black communities in the United States. In general, released inmates return to areas of highly concentrated socioeconomic disadvantage with high levels of unemployment, violence, police presence, residential instability, and family disruption (National Research Council, 2014). They may experience homelessness, compete for limited community resources, and reconnect with criminal associates that increase their risk for recidivism and reincarceration (Morenoff & Harding, 2014). Repeated contact with law enforcement and imprisonment contributes to the weakening of community stability, cohesion, and trust, including confidence in the value and fairness of the criminal justice system (LaVigne et al., 2017). This repeated contact supports legal cynicism, or the view that policing and correctional surveillance increase crime (National Research Council, 2014).

This chapter presents a systemic view of justice involvement and offender rehabilitation. It uses the key concepts of systems theory to expand on established theories of criminal conduct that inform justice interventions and to support a family-oriented approach to correctional programming. For clinicians who have an incomplete understanding of the correctional system, it also describes the components and processes of juvenile and criminal justice in the United States. This knowledge is important to appreciate the lived experiences of individuals and their relationships in diverse legal settings.

THE CRIMINAL AND JUVENILE JUSTICE SYSTEMS

Basic knowledge of the juvenile and criminal justice systems is necessary to appreciate the relations among offenders, families, and the law that influence individual behaviors. This section provides an overview of the criminal and juvenile justice systems, highlights the intersection between treatment services and the law, and describes the theories that guide justice practices and programming with a focus on institutional and community-based corrections (i.e., jail, prison, probation, and parole). Practitioners with advanced knowledge of the juvenile and criminal justice systems may find the information helpful as a refresher.

Criminal Justice

The criminal justice system consists of three branches: law enforcement, courts, and corrections. *Corrections* consists of county, state, and federal departments and agencies that form the primary site of intervention for the treatment of criminal behaviors (Krisberg et al., 2019). *Law enforcement* and *courts* operate separately and in collaboration with corrections. These three components also share a common purpose: violence prevention and public safety.

Law Enforcement and Courts

Contact with law enforcement represents a point of entry into the criminal justice system (C. L. Scott, 2010). Police officers make decisions about how to respond to crimes that vary in severity. They may issue a warning, bring the individual to a treatment facility (e.g., a hospital, an inpatient substance abuse program), or make an arrest and take the person into custody. Prosecutors decide whether to file charges with the court, and judges determine whether there is probable cause or evidence of wrongdoing. At this stage, the accused may be released on bail or held in jail until their arraignment, trial, and/or sentencing. The majority of individuals in jail (60%) are awaiting trial (Krisberg et al., 2019). When tried and convicted, offenders may return to jail to serve their sentence; be transferred to another facility (e.g., prison); or diverted to probation, depending on the severity of their crime(s) and the risk they pose to public safety.

Corrections

The corrections system is responsible for the day-to-day supervision of individuals who are arrested; detained while waiting to appear in court; charged with a crime; and sentenced to community service, probation, jail or prison. It comprises a variety of public agencies and private organizations that provide monitoring and intervention programs in the community or behind bars (Krisberg et al., 2019). The main goals of corrections are to stop criminal behaviors, hold offenders accountable, and help them become law-abiding citizens.

The term *community corrections* encompasses probation and parole, whereas *institutional corrections* refers to jail and prison. As a rule, state and federal prisons hold offenders sentenced to more than 12 months in custody, whereas jails function as a short-term or temporary detention center and clearinghouse for those awaiting trial or transfer to federal, state, or other authorities (e.g., immigration). In addition, jails are used to incarcerate probationers and parolees who have been charged with a new crime and those who have violated the terms of their probation and parole (e.g., who have failed a drug test or missed required meetings with their probation or parole officer). About 12% of probationers and 27% of parolees were sent to jail and prison in 2016 (The Pew Charitable Trusts, 2018). In general, jail facilities are near a courthouse and police headquarters, and prisons are located in remote, isolated areas. Overcrowding, lack of space, and high prisoner turnover rates are conditions that complicate treatment delivery in jails, which have an average stay of 26 days (Zeng, 2019). By contrast, prisons offer a range of programming, including education, employment, substance abuse treatment, and counseling, to address the criminogenic needs of offenders and reduce their risk of recidivism. Security in prison takes precedence over the provision of services.

Probation and *parole* are two forms of community-based supervision. When a prisoner is paroled, they are released after completing a part of their sentence behind bars, with conditions that limit their liberties (e.g., reporting to their parole officer, unannounced home visits, participating in treatment, random drug testing, curfew). Probation offers an alternative to incarceration by allowing offenders to maintain family involvement and employment under correctional supervision. It consists of regular contact with a probation officer (e.g., office meetings, home and workplace visits) and other requirements, such as mental health counseling and family therapy. Compared with prison and jail, parole and probation place greater emphasis on the principles of offender rehabilitation. However, since the 1980s, they have adopted a law-and-order approach to monitoring that emphasizes punishment for low-level offenses or technical violations of correctional supervision (Krisberg et al., 2019).

Problem-Solving Courts

Mental illness, homelessness, and drug and alcohol abuse are some of the social and public health issues that lead to involvement with the criminal justice system. In the past 40 years, the criminalization of these complex problems—drug use in particular—has resulted in increased arrest rates, congested court dockets, delays in case processing, and overcrowded jails and prisons. *Problem-solving courts* are intended to be a solution to the clogging of the criminal justice system. They constitute an innovative legal approach to the management of nonviolent low-level offenders who present a variety of concerns, such as mental illness and drug or alcohol addiction. They are an alternative to incarceration and a strategy for linking adult and juvenile offenders with community-based services (Strong et al., 2016).

In 2020, there were 4,168 problem-solving courts in the United States; 30% were adult drug treatment courts, and 10.8% were mental health courts (National Drug Court Resource Center, n.d.). Problem-solving courts represent efforts to integrate the justice and human services systems. Their purpose is to deal with the causes of criminal behaviors more effectively, using legal authority and systems of rewards and sanctions to get defendants to enter and stay in treatment (Boldt, 2009). Problem-solving courts use surveillance and behavior control strategies (e.g., regular drug testing, court appearances) to hold offenders accountable. They require offenders to participate in programming (e.g., addiction treatment, counseling, life skills training, anger management) that will increase their ability to create positive lifestyle changes (Berman, 2009). Failure to comply with the conditions of the court results in some form of punishment, such as community service and jail stay.

Problem-solving courts share common principles (Berman, 2009). They emphasize the use of advanced information about addiction and mental illness, for example, to better understand offenders' criminal behaviors and improve sentencing and treatment decisions. They seek to develop collaborative partnerships with key stakeholders and community agencies as well as citizens and communities who have been afflicted with the problem. They also promote individualized and evidence-based justice interventions that match the needs of each participant and include outcome monitoring. In problem-solving courts, the judge directs the treatment team, which may consist of probation officers, law enforcement, service providers, prosecutors, and public defenders. The judge coordinates treatment, monitors offenders' progress toward the program goals, and interacts directly with the participants during status hearings. Offenders typically must plead guilty before entering the program, and the average number of participants ranges from 10 to 49, depending on the type of problem-solving court (Strong et al., 2016).

Juvenile Justice

The separation of youth and adults in the criminal justice system dates back to the mid-19th century, with the creation of the first privately run facilities for juvenile offenders, followed by the establishment of the first juvenile court in 1899. Juvenile justice developed from the understanding that childhood and adolescence were periods of critical cognitive development. It was also founded on the basis of the belief that the state was responsible for the welfare of children whose parents were not able to care for them; this is also referred as the *parens patriae doctrine* (OJJDP, 1999). Today, a majority of states (29 of 50) have adopted a balanced and restorative approach to juvenile justice (the BARJ model; OJJDP, 2016). The BARJ model emphasizes offender accountability; skill development; public safety; and the participation of victims, offenders, and communities in repairing harm (OJJDP, 1997). In essence, the primary goal of juvenile justice is rehabilitation with sentencing and interventions focused on the needs of the person rather than the type of crime committed. However, since the 1990s, punishment and deterrence have resurfaced as a preferred response to juvenile crime and have often eclipsed efforts to educate and treat delinquent youth to become productive and law-abiding citizens (OJJDP, 1999).

The operations of the juvenile justice system are governed by local laws and therefore vary by state. In general, the police are the first point of contact with the juvenile justice system. When parents, schools, social service agencies, or victims report a delinquent act, law enforcement decides how to best handle the case (National Research Council & Institute of Medicine, 2001): whether to refer the youth for further assessment, file a delinquency petition, or divert the youth to an informal adjustment program. *Informal adjustment* consists of activities (e.g., community service, family counseling) approved by the juvenile court and monitored by the juvenile court probation department. Diversion away from the juvenile justice system can occur at any point during the processing of a delinquency case: at intake or during adjudication (similar to adult conviction) and disposition (equivalent to adult sentencing). When the youth is found delinquent, they may be court ordered to probation supervision in the community or to a secure correctional placement. As a rule, both probation supervision and detention plans include the requirement to participate in treatment services such as mental health assessment and counseling.

PSYCHOLOGY IN AMERICAN CORRECTIONS

Corrections is a system designed to protect the public from crime and violence using incapacitation, deterrence, retribution, and rehabilitation as primary methods of intervention (Krisberg et al., 2019). *Incapacitation* is the limitation of individual freedoms through imprisonment, community supervision, and other legal requirements that control individual movement. *Deterrence* is based on the belief that punishment and the threat of punishment can stop people from offending when the costs of crime outweigh the benefits. *Retribution* corresponds to punishment; it is the consequence or penalty society imposes on offenders for doing harm. "Do the crime, do the time" is the catchphrase of retributive justice in the United States. Last, *rehabilitation* refers to a set of educational, counseling, and other activities that target individual, relational, and social factors linked to criminal behaviors, with the goal of transforming offenders into law-abiding citizens.

The Risk-Need-Responsivity Model

The risk–need–responsivity (RNR) model of offender rehabilitation is the dominant theoretical and psychological framework of correctional practice in the United States (Andrews & Bonta, 2015; National Institute of Corrections, 2004). It offers a set of principles for integrating clinical and social services in justice settings and for assessing and treating offenders to address the major causes of crime. The principles of the RNR model are derived from the research findings of the psychology of criminal conduct (PCC; Bonta, 2019) approach. PCC is both a science and a conceptual approach to understanding crime; it integrates elements of behavioral, personality, and cognitive theories in a general personality and cognitive social learning model of criminal conduct. In PCC, offending is a learned behavior acquired through modeling and conditioning, classical and operant, and influenced by intrapersonal and environmental factors; specifically, PCC emphasizes the role of antisocial personality patterns and procriminal attitudes as individual variables that explain crime (Andrews & Bonta, 2015; Bonta, 2019). Impulsivity, risk taking, pleasure seeking, aggressivity, and callous disregard for others are the characteristics that define antisocial personality patterns. *Procriminal attitudes* are thoughts, beliefs, and feelings that support lawbreaking behaviors (e.g., taking pride in criminal acts, rejecting prosocial institutions and norms).

The RNR model posits that it is possible to predict who will engage in criminal activities and reoffend or recidivate (Andrews & Bonta, 2015). Meta-analyses and longitudinal studies have identified several covariates or predictive factors of criminal conduct. These are categorized into four types:

1. *Risk factors*: personal characteristics or external conditions that increase the likelihood of future criminal acts.
2. *Criminogenic needs*: dynamic risk factors that are amenable to change through targeted interventions to reduce recidivism. Chapter 3 provides an in-depth review of the empirical literature on the criminogenic needs linked to offending.
3. *Noncriminogenic needs*: variables that are not directly associated with criminal conduct and therefore are not typically the focus of correctional programming.
4. *Strengths*: protective or resilience factors that reduce the likelihood of recidivism.

Empirical evidence suggests there are eight well-known predictive factors of criminal conduct (Andrews & Bonta, 2015). Among them, four are defined as major causes or sources of variation: (a) history of antisocial behavior, (b) antisocial personality pattern, (c) antisocial cognition, and (d) antisocial associates. These are called the "Big Four" and are linked to specific change goals, such as building self-control, anger management, and problem-solving skills and cognitive restructuring to reduce procriminal attitudes and promote affiliation with prosocial groups and institutions.

In the RNR model, the characteristics of the family environment have a moderate relation to criminal behaviors (Andrews & Bonta, 2015). The emphasis is on the quality of the family and marital relationships (mutual caring, respect, and interest), parenting practices (level of parental nurturance and supervision during adolescence), and family expectations and rules about behaviors. PCC recognizes that the family is central in the development and maintenance of criminal conduct (Bonta, 2019): It is the site of early socialization, whereby children observe and learn behaviors that are either appropriate or inappropriate and where they get rewarded or disciplined for acting aggressively and not complying with social norms. In adulthood, the strength of couple and family relationships may influence how individuals evaluate the costs and rewards of crime (e.g., the pain of being incarcerated and separated from significant others and children). Couples may also interact in ways that reinforce procriminal attitudes and behaviors.

Together with (a) the family, (b) school and work, (c) participation in prosocial leisure activities, and (d) substance abuse are the four moderate risk factors of the RNR model. Family, school, work, and leisure activities are relational contexts in which interactions form the contingencies (antecedents and consequences, rewards and costs) of individual actions, including crime (Andrews & Bonta, 2015). PCC emphasizes a cognitive behavioral understanding of the relation between offending and social contexts: Antisocial cognitions, which are linked to negative emotional states about others, beget antisocial behaviors that produce problematic responses from the environment (see Figure 1.1). When the relational context consists of associates or relatives that share procriminal attitudes, the probability is high that their reactions will support criminal cognitions and activities and increase the likelihood of reoffending.

The strength of PCC, which is the foundation of the RNR model, lies in the integration of psychological science and theories to explain variation in criminal conduct between and within individuals over time. Correctional interventions that follow the RNR principles have been found to produce greater reductions in recidivism compared with other types of programs (Andrews & Bonta, 2015; Looman & Abracen, 2013). Despite these positive outcomes, the RNR model has been criticized for putting too much emphasis on personal deficits and the management and reduction of risk factors at the expense of individual strengths, values, goals, self-concept, and agency (Barnao et al., 2015; Looman & Abracen, 2013). Ward et al. (2007) proposed an alternative approach to offender rehabilitation that integrates the principles of humanistic and positive psychology: the good lives model (GLM).

FIGURE 1.1. The Relation Between Person and Context in the Psychology of Criminal Conduct Approach

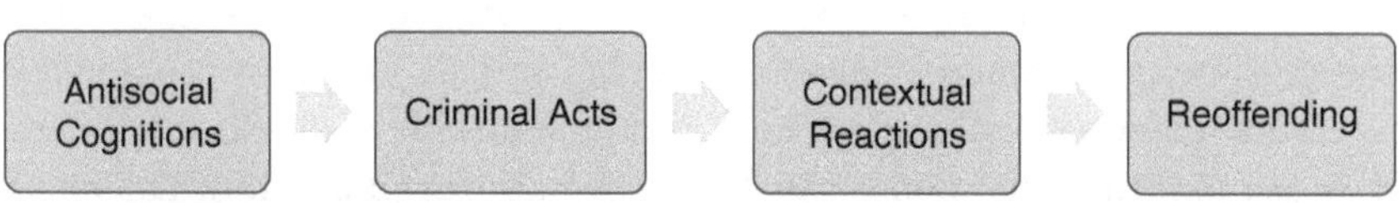

The Good Lives Model

The GLM is a general conceptual framework that specifies the aims of correctional interventions as well as the pathways to change, with an emphasis on human agency and autonomy in decision making (Ward, 2011; Ward et al., 2007). It is based on a set of assumptions about human nature and individual action. First, behaviors are purposeful and are directed toward obtaining primary goods, or conditions, characteristics, and experiences that promote psychological well-being and a good, meaningful, and fulfilling life. There are 11 categories of primary goods, among them *friendship*, which refers to a person's social bonds, including intimate, romantic, and family relationships. The GLM also highlights individuals' capacity for adaptation using internal and external tools and the role of identity or self-concept in offender rehabilitation. There is a reciprocal relation between a person's sense of who they are, what they value, and how they act. For this reason, GLM programming aims to facilitate the development of positive social identities at the same time as they help offenders build the skills and resources needed to control criminogenic factors and pursue primary goods such as health, knowledge, and social connection. Last, the GLM recognizes the interdependent relation between people and their social settings. GLM interventions are tailored to take into consideration the characteristics of offenders' environment and increase their ability to manage risk and build positive and prosocial lives in their specific context.

A FAMILY SYSTEMS APPROACH TO OFFENDER REHABILITATION

Both the GLM and the RNR model of rehabilitation include some attention to the family system. From the RNR perspective, the family of origin is the context in which antisocial attitudes and behaviors develop and become established patterns of individual action in response to environmental deficits (e.g., poor parental monitoring, inconsistent discipline) and mechanisms of reinforcement (e.g., rewards). In adulthood, the quality of couple and family relationships moderates how offenders experience the costs of criminal conduct (e.g., conflict with significant others, separation, loss). The GLM views couple and family relationships—relatedness in particular—as a source of motivation and a behavioral goal (Ward, 2011). Most people seek to create a sense of belonging; how they pursue this goal and the means they use to form social bonds can be problematic, even harmful. The focus of the GLM on personal identities also constitutes an opportunity to examine the family system, in particular the effects of family roles and family structure on offending.

Family involvement in offender rehabilitation is to be expected because all individuals belong to some form of kinship systems. Family involvement can take various forms: It may consist of direct and/or indirect contact with law enforcement, the court, and the correctional system; it may or may not be legally mandated. For example, family members may attend court hearings, visit their relative behind bars, deposit money on the offender's commissary account, and pay his or her legal fees. They may provide transportation to probation or parole meetings, write letters to the judge, and speak with the probation officer when that officer visits the home of the offender. They may ask the offender questions about their probation or parole meetings and participate in treatment programs as ordered by the court. Family involvement is also psychological and emotional and manifested in worries and negativity.

This section expands on the conceptualization of the family in the RNR model and the GLM and lays the foundation for the next chapters. It describes the core concepts and principles of family systems theory and discusses how these concepts and principles can enhance our understanding of couple and family relationship processes in offender rehabilitation. Couples and families constitute relational contexts of face-to-face communication and interaction. The family is also a system that has several roles in society (Carr, 2016): to socialize children, transmit norms, regulate individual activities, and provide practical and emotional support. Considering its social functions, the family represents a critical site of intervention in rehabilitative programming.

Family Systems Theory

Contemporary systems thinking integrates elements of bioecological and transactional models of human development (Fiese et al., 2019; Stanton & Welsh, 2011). It offers a holistic view of the person with a focus on the interplay among individual, relational, and contextual/macrosystemic factors that influence well-being (Stanton, 2009). *Individual factors* include interconnected and dynamic biological, cognitive, and emotional processes that occur within the person. *Relational factors* are those characteristics and patterns that define couple, family, and other social systems whereby individuals interact with others. *Contextual and macrosystemic factors* encompass aspects of the broader environment, such as the neighborhood, religious group, and culture in which individuals are embedded. Time is also an important dimension of human behavior; it refers to the normative (e.g., becoming parents) and nonnormative (e.g., incarceration) transitions of the life cycle as well as historical changes that affect individual and family functioning (Ferguson & Evans, 2019).

Reciprocity

Table 1.1 shows that the risk and need factors of the RNR model and the primary goods of the GLM fall into two of the dimensions just described: (a) individual and (b) relational. From a systemic perspective, these factors are not discrete but interdependent elements organized into complex living systems whose interactions influence criminal behaviors (Stanton, 2009). It is the reciprocal relations among individual, interpersonal, and contextual factors that promote the development and maintenance of antisocial patterns in particular circumstances. *Complexity* and *reciprocity* are core concepts of systems theory; they are linked to the ideas of nonsummativity and circular causality, which emphasize the patterns that connect as well as the components

TABLE 1.1. Classification of the Risk-Need-Responsivity (RNR) Model and Good Lives Model (GLM) Factors

Model	Individual factors	Relational factors
RNR	Antisocial behaviors (history of) Personality patterns • Impulsivity • Negative emotionality (anger, irritability, aggressivity) • Sensation seeking Antisocial cognition • Procriminal attitudes, values, and beliefs • Cognitive processes (e.g., rationalizing criminal behaviors) • Self-concept or personal identity that support offending Substance abuse	Antisocial associates (negative peer influence) Family/marital circumstances School/work (relationships and performance)
GLM	Healthy living Knowledge Mastery Autonomy and self-directedness Emotional self-regulation Spirituality Happiness Creativity	Friendships Family relationships Intimate relationships

that make up the whole (Stanton, 2009). These patterns are nonlinear; they develop from the components' interactions and mutual influence.

Looking at Table 1.1 with a systemic lens entails that one examine the mutual effects of individual and interpersonal factors: for example, how negative emotionality interacts with procriminal beliefs and values in the context of family conflict and how neighborhood violence influences the relation among family conflict, antisocial cognition, and negative emotionality. The person is a system defined by internal and interdependent biological, emotional, cognitive, and behavioral processes that is nested in or in relation with broader systems such as the family, the local community, and social institutions. For example, criminal behaviors may influence, and be influenced by, low family and neighborhood cohesion and the interactions among the family, the neighborhood, and law enforcement (C. M. Thompson, Datchi, & Eure, in press).

Adaptation

During their transactions, the person, the family, and broader social systems continuously exchange information and resources. The term *adaptation* describes the concept of openness in systems theory (Carr, 2016; Stanton, 2009). Openness is necessary for human social systems to adapt to new circumstances, reorganize and respond to internal and external demands for change, and continue to operate in the face of developmental and other challenges. Criminal justice involvement is a stressor that puts pressure on the family system to restructure and redistribute roles, responsibilities, and resources (Datchi, Barretti, & Thompson, 2016). For example, the incarceration of a relative may result in lost income, if that individual had contributed money to the family finances. Likewise, family members may assume more responsibility for child care to help their relative meet the requirements of their probation.

Family Structure

The structure of family systems influences couple and family functioning as well as individuals' capacity to achieve the primary goods of the GLM, such as healthy living, emotional self-regulation, and warm and affectionate bonds. The *family structure* corresponds to a set of rules that organize individual behaviors and interpersonal transactions within and between the family system and subsystems (e.g., within the spousal subsystem and between parents and children; Minuchin, 1974). These rules determine who belongs to the family system and subsystems and define the purpose of the family system and subsystems and the roles of each family member. They also specify individuals' power or degree of influence in dyadic relationships. For example, the purpose of the parental subsystem is to provide care and safety for the children. To carry out this function, parents use their position of authority in the family system, which changes over time. They may also develop complementary roles in their efforts to work as a team.

The structure of family systems varies on three dimensions of functioning: (a) cohesion, (b) flexibility, and (c) communication (Olson & Gorall, 2003). *Cohesion* corresponds to the level of togetherness and emotional bonding between individual family members; *flexibility* refers to the family system's ability to balance stability and change in leadership, roles, and rules; and *communication* is the process by which families achieve cohesion and flexibility. These three dimensions are involved in the development of individual distress: Hostile couple communication has been linked to negative health outcomes, including a higher risk of cardiovascular diseases, mood and anxiety disorders, and pain-related disability (Repetti & Saxbe, 2019). Likewise, perceived and expressed criticism, negativity, and emotional overinvolvement in family relationships are associated with higher rates of relapse for individuals with severe mental illness, such as bipolar disorder or schizophrenia (Whisman, 2019).

Family Resilience

A family systems approach to offender rehabilitation emphasizes the relational contexts of individual behaviors as a site of intervention to support the person's engagement in prosocial family roles and activities and stimulate *family resilience* as a buffer against risk (Datchi, 2017a). The aim is to interrupt and change the family transactions that are involved in the maintenance of criminogenic individual patterns, such as negative emotionality and substance misuse (see Table 1.1). The focus is on the extended family system's resilience factors that empower family members to come together and gather resources to overcome adversity and maintain optimal functioning (Harrist et al., 2019; Walsh, 2012). Family resilience involves positive adaptation and growth (Walsh, 2012). Henry et al. (2015)'s model of family resilience provides a sophisticated framework for the assessment of family processes that facilitate positive adaptation to the stressful conditions of criminal justice involvement. From a family systems perspective, it is those processes that have the potential, when activated, to support offenders in their pursuit of healthy living, happiness, self-directedness, or mastery.

Macrosystemic Factors

A family systems approach to offender rehabilitation involves knowledge and understanding of the individual diversity and macrosystemic factors that influence clinical problems (Stanton & Welsh, 2011). Criminal behaviors alone do not explain the nearly four-fold increase in the number of justice-involved individuals since the 1980s: Rates of victimization have declined gradually after reaching a peak in the late 1980s (Mears & Cochran, 2015). In 2015, the number of violent and property crimes was 50% lower than in 1991 (National Criminal Justice Reference Service, 2017). To understand the dramatic growth of the correctional population, it is important to consider broader systemic factors: legal, political, and social.

The expansion of American corrections corresponds to the country's renewed emphasis on punishment, incapacitation, and deterrence, rather than rehabilitation, as strategies to reduce and prevent crime (Mears & Cochran, 2015). It also follows from legal reforms that have criminalized public health and social problems, such as drug use and poverty. In the early 1980s, federal policies introduced new sentencing guidelines that required stiffer penalties for drug law violations, including substance use (Mauer & King, 2007). From 1990 to 2010, the number of arrests for drug possession or use increased by 80% (H. N. Snyder, 2012). In 2018, the majority (86.4%) of drug arrests were for possession of illicit substances (Federal Bureau of Investigation, 2019). The legal reforms of the 1980s also imposed longer prison sentences for drug offenses and fueled the rise of incarceration rates. From 1980 to 2017, there was an 11-fold increase in the number of inmates with drug use disorders. In 2004, these individuals served an average sentence of 62 months in prison (The Sentencing Project, 2021).

Like drug use, poverty, mental illness, and undocumented immigration status increase the likelihood of criminal justice involvement. Sleeping in public places and panhandling may lead to fines, probation supervision, or/and jail time in cities that ban these behaviors (Dolan, 2015). When poor people are unable to pay their debts, they also are at greater risk for incarceration. Failure to pay required probation or parole fees, for example, is considered a technical violation and may be grounds for detention. In 2019, technical violations represented one in four new admissions in state prisons (The Pew Charitable Trusts, 2019). The criminalization of mental illness is evidenced by the rates of psychiatric disorders in correctional populations. According to the U.S. Department of Justice (2009), these are 3 to 6 times greater than in the general public. Where access to appropriate treatment is limited or not available, the criminal justice system has stepped in and played a greater role in managing behaviors associated with disabilities and mental health conditions (Rifkin, 2017). Last, beginning in the 1990s, law enforcement and correction have become key actors in the enforcement of U.S. immigration policies, from arrest to conviction and punishment.

In 2011, immigration violations were the most prevalent types of federal crimes, above drug offenses. Sentences for unlawful entry in the United States range from a fine and a few months in jail to several years in prison. The convergence of criminal and immigration law has contributed to the definition of undocumented immigrants as "illegal aliens" and their growing involvement with the U.S. criminal justice system.

Schools are often the first site where youth come in contact with the juvenile justice system, through their interactions with the police or school resource officer and through punitive disciplinary actions that include suspension, expulsion, and referral to juvenile courts for disorderly conduct (Nelson & Lind, 2015). Since the early 1990s, U.S. schools have taken a zero-tolerance approach to discipline and safety. In the early 1990s, U.S. schools adopted a zero-tolerance approach to discipline and safety, which resulted in a 10% increase in out-of-school suspension (Nelson & Lind, 2015). Zero-tolerance policies were originally intended to manage serious offenses, such as selling drugs on school grounds; however, they have been used to address minor misbehaviors, such as talking back to teachers or skipping class. These policies have had a differential impact on Black students and students with disabilities who have experienced school-related arrests at disproportionate rates compared with White and able-bodied students (U.S. Department of Education Office for Civil Rights, 2014).

In sum, justice involvement is the product of various diversity and macrosystemic factors: legal reforms, school policies, economic disadvantages, racial biases, and lack of treatment resources for drug abuse and mental illness in the community. Punishment, deterrence, and incapacitation are legal strategies that emphasize individual responsibility and agency. To effectively tackle the problem of crime, however, it is important to understand the complex relations among individual behaviors, family relationships, and the environment.

CONCLUSION

This chapter has presented information that shows the scope of individuals' involvement with the juvenile and criminal justice systems and the far-reaching impact that those systems have on the everyday life of families and communities. It has provided a broad description of the juvenile and criminal justice systems to clarify how people enter and move through their various arenas. It has argued that family involvement is a critical and obvious component of correctional programming. Last, it has discussed a family systems approach to offender rehabilitation that incorporates the core concepts of contemporary systems thinking, including knowledge and understanding of how intrapersonal, relational, contextual, and diversity factors interact with one another to shape the experience of individuals, couples, and families.

Chapter 2 introduces a case study; expands on the issue of individual and cultural diversity; and examines how race, ethnicity, gender, age, education level, employment status, and mental health define the experience of justice-involved individuals and families.

2 CORRECTIONAL POPULATIONS IN THE UNITED STATES

Diversity Factors

Knowledge of individual and cultural diversity is a core element of professional competence in clinical practice (Stanton & Welsh, 2011). Individual and cultural diversity factors shape how individuals, couples, and families define and address difficulties and how they experience and engage in treatment (Casas, 2017; C. C. Lee, 2013). This chapter highlights salient diversity factors in U.S. corrections that emerge from a review of recent justice statistics: race, ethnicity, gender, socioeconomic, and mental health disparities. It is not intended to discuss racial, gender, and class biases and discrimination in the juvenile and criminal justice systems; there are many publications that center on this topic (e.g., Burling, 2018; Datchi & Ancis, 2017). Instead, the goal is to draw attention to key conditions, psychological and contextual, that influence the lived experiences of individuals, couples, and families. Research linking diversity factors to delinquency and crime are discussed in Chapter 3.

This chapter opens with the story of a fictitious family: Sam, Sara, Julia, and Gabriel, who personify the various challenges associated with justice involvement. The book follows the family in the justice system and in

https://doi.org/10.1037/0000285-003
Best Clinical Practices for Treating Families in Juvenile and Criminal Justice Systems, by C. C. Datchi

treatment. After introducing the family, the chapter presents information about salient diversity factors in U.S. corrections. Next, it shows how to use this knowledge to identify areas of multicultural assessment that are important to explore with the fictitious family, in order to understand the effects of social disadvantages and systemic oppression on their individual and relational functioning.

PORTRAIT OF A JUSTICE-INVOLVED FAMILY

Sam and Sara met when they were 18. They have two children: Gabriel, age 15; and Julia, age 17. Sara and the children live in a low-income urban neighborhood where the population is predominantly immigrant, Black, and Latino and where public safety and drugs are concerns. Sam is in jail at present for violating the conditions of his parole: He tested positive for marijuana use. He is now waiting to appear before the parole board. If Sam is released back to the community, he intends to live with Sara and the children. The couple have had an on-and-off relationship over the years. They became engaged a few weeks before Sam's current incarceration.

Sam is a 36-year-old Latino Black man born in the United States to working-class, Dominican parents. His involvement with the U.S. criminal justice system dates back to adolescence, when he was first arrested for possession and distribution of controlled dangerous substance at age 14. Sam's criminal history as a juvenile and adult offender includes school fights, truancy, criminal possession of a weapon, drug sale, physical assault, and robbery with a firearm. At age 16, Sam was ordered to juvenile detention, where he completed cognitive behavioral and substance education programs. Since then, he has remained under some form of correctional supervision: jail, probation, drug treatment court, prison, and parole. While in juvenile detention, Sam developed vocational skills and earned a high school degree. Back in the community, he joined his family's construction business, where he was paid minimum wage under the table. In between jail and prison, he continued to work in the family business.

Sam's drug of choice is marijuana. He has been using substances since he was 12. Prior to his present incarceration, he smoked four to five blunts of marijuana and drank two to five bottles of beer daily. He also snorted cocaine and abused anxiolytics occasionally. In addition to substance use problems, Sam was diagnosed with posttraumatic stress disorder (PTSD). Through childhood, adolescence, and adulthood, he was exposed to multiple traumatic events: At age 5, he witnessed the shooting of his father during a police raid; at age 17, he saw the killing of his best friend; he was also involved in violent gang-related fights behind bars.

Sam was selling drugs on the streets when he met Sara, who is now age 34, a White woman who immigrated from Portugal at age 7, with her parents and two siblings. Sara works day and evening shifts as a registered nurse in a community hospital. Given the costs of Sam's involvement in the criminal justice system, she has been the primary provider and parent for her two children. With the exception of her mother, Diana, she receives little support from her family members, who disapprove of her association with Sam. Shortly after her son was born, she stopped going to her family's Catholic church, and joined her neighborhood's Baptist congregation, where she finds material and spiritual assistance. Sara describes her Christian faith as a source of comfort and strength.

Sara has a history of alcohol and marijuana use. She stopped smoking marijuana when her daughter was born. She drinks two to three bottles of beer every day to relieve stress and go to sleep. Her only involvement with the criminal justice system is through Sam and her son, Gabriel, who was arrested and placed on informal probation at age 15, for underage drinking and fights in and out of school. Sara worries about her ability to manage her children's behaviors, about protecting her children from the neighborhood's criminal activities, and about the impact of Sam's multiple incarcerations. In particular, Sara is concerned about Gabriel, who puts his father on a pedestal and brags about Sam's street smarts and involvement in the criminal justice system.

Sara does her best to monitor and discipline Gabriel; however, single parenthood and variability in work hours make it hard to provide ongoing parental supervision and maintain consistent family routines. Limited economic resources are another source of stress. Sara and Gabriel often argue about truancy, academic performance, and peers. On several occasions, their arguments escalated negatively: Gabriel has broken a window and run away from home twice in the past 6 months.

Gabriel's behaviors have aroused the attention of his teachers and guidance counselor, who recommended a psychological evaluation. The school psychologist diagnosed Gabriel with emotional disturbance and cognitive deficits that interfered with his ability to read and process information. An individualized education program was established to meet Gabriel's educational needs; however, his behaviors have not improved: He skips school, fights, and drinks alcohol with his peers almost every day. He was recently suspended for swearing at a teacher and being under the influence of alcohol. The school principal has met with Sara to discuss the probability of expulsion.

Like his father, Gabriel has witnessed many traumatic events since early childhood that involved physical assaults and gun violence. He shows signs of irritability and anger and has spoken to Sara about having nightmares. Since he entered middle school, Gabriel has stopped all extracurricular activities; he no longer enjoys playing soccer and basketball and spends most of his time with substance-using peers.

Both Gabriel and Julia attend public schools where overcrowding, limited educational resources, gang violence, and drugs are significant concerns. Julia is on the honor roll and participates in many after-school activities. She takes ballet classes, leads her school's book club, and volunteers in a nursing home. She has received praise from her teachers for her good grades and exemplary attitude in the classroom. Julia feels embarrassed about her father's incarceration; she has told her friends Sam is serving in the army and comes home only for Thanksgiving and Christmas. Two months ago, she started smoking marijuana with her new boyfriend. She has been using once a week to help her relax. Last week, she received school detention for tardiness and failure to complete her work.

The family's relationships are distant and conflictual. Julia and Gabriel have separate groups of friends and talk only during mealtimes on the weekend. They share little information with Sara, who does not know they are drinking or smoking marijuana. Once a week, Sara, Julia, and Gabriel visit Sam in the jail and talk with him on the phone. Phone conversations between Sara and Sam are fraught with friction, criticism, and defensiveness: When Sara expresses mistrust in Sam's ability to be reliable and honest, he falls silent. Before his present incarceration, the couple often argued about Sam's past infidelity. Sara would search his phone for evidence that he was sexting other women, and Sam would get angry, tell Sara she was out of control and crazy, and walk away from their unresolved and perpetual conflict. Sara saw Sam as unemotional and distant; she felt rejected. Sam perceived Sara as demanding and irrational; he felt overwhelmed with her perceived emotional instability. However, the couple was committed to staying together and keeping their family intact.

CAUGHT IN THE NET: THE ROLE OF DIVERSITY FACTORS

About two thirds of individuals with a history of incarceration are caught in the net of the criminal justice system. Recidivism and rearrest rates of prisoners are noticeably high, ranging from 68% at 3 years after release to 83% at 9 years afterward (Alper et al., 2018; Gelb & Velázquez, 2018).

Recidivism is a legal term that refers to a person's return to criminal behaviors within 3 years of completing their sanctions behind bars or in the community (National Institute of Justice, n.d.-b). Recidivism rates, however, include the number of offenders incarcerated for a technical violation of probation or parole (e.g., failing to report for a scheduled visit, testing positive for drugs) as well as those rearrested for a new crime (The Pew Center on the States, 2011). These rates say something about the impediments (e.g., restricted access to housing, employment, mental health services, and social services) that make it difficult for returning citizens to achieve a "good life" in the community free from correctional supervision (Mears & Cochran, 2015). In particular, the first 12 months after release are a critical period when individuals are at very high risk for relapse and when they need formal and informal assistance to become productive members of their families and communities (Durose et al., 2014).

The following paragraphs review information about diversity factors, including disparities in mental health, that contribute to chronic justice involvement. Data about race and ethnicity, gender, psychiatric disorders, education, and employment highlight the psychological, social, and economic disadvantages of individuals and families who are entangled with the juvenile and criminal justice systems. To understand the concerns of correctional populations and address their needs, it is necessary to conduct a contextual assessment and to consider how their environment determines their behavioral, relational, and social outcomes (Stanton & Welsh, 2011). A contextual assessment also highlights areas for advocacy to remove external barriers to well-being and support patient progress in treatment.

Race and Ethnicity

Although racial and ethnic disparities in U.S. corrections have declined since 2000 (Sabol et al., 2019), between-group differences remain visible. For example, in 2016, the number of sentenced Black men behind bars was almost 6 times higher than the number of non-Hispanic White men (Bronson & Carson, 2019). This racial disparity ratio was greater for young Black males (age 18 and 19), who were 12 times more likely to be incarcerated than their White counterparts (Bronson & Carson, 2019). Likewise, in 2016, the parole rates for Blacks were about 4 times higher than those for Whites (Sabol et al., 2019). One in 23 Black adults were on probation or parole, compared with one in 81 White adults (Horowitz & Utada, 2018). From 2000 to 2016, the Black-to-White ratio of female inmates decreased from 6:1 to 2:1 (Sabol et al., 2019). During the same period, the ratio of Hispanic to White parolees and prisoners declined from 3.1:1 to 1.5:1 and from 2.5:1 to 1.6:1, respectively. In 2017, the incarceration rates for Black and Hispanic women ages 18 to 19 were about 4.5 and 2 times higher than for White women (Bronson & Carson, 2019). More recent statistics suggest there were no differences in representation between Whites and Hispanics on probation in 2016 (Sabol et al., 2019); however, this trend may reflect missing data from states that do not report information about offenders' ethnicity (Horowitz & Utada, 2018).

Juvenile justice statistics show similar racial and ethnic disparities among juvenile offenders. In 2017, White youth accounted for approximately 85% of the U.S. juvenile population and 44% of all delinquency cases; the rates for Black youth were 15.3% and 35%, respectively (Hockenberry, 2019). Between-group differences were visible at each stage of the judicial process: Black youth represented the majority of referrals to juvenile courts (61.8% compared with 21% for Whites and 19.9% for Hispanics); they also had the highest rate of petitions for formal processing (63% compared with 52% for Whites and 59% for Hispanics) and the highest percentage of judicial waivers to adult criminal court (54% compared with 31% for Whites and 12% for Hispanics; Hockenberry & Puzzanchera, 2019). When adjudicated, 32% and 33% of cases involving Black and Hispanic youth received a sanction of confinement compared with 22% for Whites. White male youth were more likely than Blacks and Hispanics to be placed on formal probation (Hockenberry, 2019).

Gender

Men and boys account for the majority of the U.S. justice population. Women make up a smaller yet growing proportion of individuals under correctional supervision. In 2017, they represented 7% of the total number of prisoners (Bronson & Carson, 2019); this percentage was almost 8 times higher than in 1980 (The Sentencing Project, 2021). Likewise, there has been a twofold increase in the number of women on probation and parole since 1990. By year-end 2016, 1 million women were supervised in the community; they represented one quarter of the total probation population and one in eight parolees (Horowitz & Utada, 2018).

The latest survey of the U.S. inmate population showed that the majority of men (51%–63%) and women (56%–62%) reported having at least one child (Glaze & Maruschak, 2008). Black prisoners accounted for more than four in 10 fathers behind bars, compared with three in 10 for Whites and two in 10 for Hispanics; more than half (48%) of all mothers in prison were

White (Glaze & Maruschak, 2008). In 2007, mothers represented two thirds of the female population behind bars, and the majority (77%) were responsible for their children's daily care before detention.

Overall, the proportion of girls in the juvenile justice system has remained stable, at 27% to 28% (Hockenberry, 2019). In 2015, female youth age 17 or less represented less than one third of all juvenile arrests and fewer than four in 10 delinquency cases (Ehrmann et al., 2019). Most female delinquency cases (53%) were referred or diverted to rehabilitation programs before adjudication, compared with 42% of male delinquency cases (Ehrmann et al., 2019). The majority of justice-involved girls were age 15 and older (67%) and members of a racial–ethnic minority group (35% Black and 17% Hispanic; Ehrmann et al., 2019). Black girls were the only overrepresented group in the juvenile justice system (35% vs. 15% in the U.S. population); in addition, they were about 3 times more likely than White and Hispanic girls to be referred to juvenile court (Ehrmann et al., 2019). A higher number of adjudicated Hispanic female youth were ordered to detention and out-of-home placement (e.g., treatment, foster care).

Education Level

Most studies of educational attainment in U.S. correctional populations have focused on incarcerated adults (Couloute, 2018; Duke, 2018; Ewert & Wildhagen, 2011; Tofig, 2017). The findings suggest that male and female inmates of all ages have lower levels of education than their counterparts in the general public, are less likely to have graduated high school and completed some college, and are more likely to report a high school equivalency certificate as their highest educational achievement (Ewert & Wildhagen, 2011). Researchers estimate that 37% to 58% of prisoners did not finish high school, compared with 14% to 15% of the general population; 60% of formerly incarcerated individuals have a general equivalency diploma (GED) certificate, compared with 4% to 10% of the public; and about three quarters of those individuals earned a GED behind bars (Couloute, 2018; Ewert & Wildhagen, 2011). Less than 10% of individuals who got a GED in prison will complete some higher education, and less than 1% will graduate with a college degree. Similar trends have been reported for probation populations, with a high school dropout rate of 31% (Wolf Harlow, 2003). In addition, research has found gender and racial differences in education attainment (Duke, 2018): Before incarceration, men have lower levels of education than women and, compared with White, Hispanic, and female offenders, Black men who had completed only high school represent a higher proportion of the U.S. correctional populations.

Employment

Employment and income level are associated with educational attainment. Postincarceration unemployment rates for offenders without a high school degree range from 25% for White men to 60% for Black women (Couloute, 2018). Overall unemployment rates for correctional populations range from 18.4% for White men to 43.6% for Black women; they are about 5 times above the figures for the general public (4.3% for White men and 6.4% for Black women; Couloute & Kopf, 2018). In 2014, former inmates reported median yearly earnings of $10,090 in the first 12 months after release (Looney & Turner, 2018). Economic disadvantage predated incarceration, with employment rates of 49% and median annual earnings of $6,250 in the 3 years before detention (Looney & Turner, 2018).

Family poverty is a predictor of incarceration. It intersects with gender and race and has a differential impact for diverse communities. Boys and girls born to families in the lowest income brackets are 40 and 17 times more likely to go to prison during adulthood compared with boys and girls born to the wealthiest families (Looney & Turner, 2018). The risk of incarceration is highest among Black and Native American men who grew up in segregated, urban neighborhoods and Indian reservations with high rates of child poverty, single-parent households, and unemployment (Looney & Turner, 2018).

The family environment is a source of financial support for formerly incarcerated individuals. When they return to their communities, most prisoners (79%) spend time looking for work. A minority (31%) are employed 2 months after release, and their median hourly wages are about $8 (Visher et al., 2011). Almost half rely on the financial assistance of their relatives and friends in the first 8 months after release. Research findings indicate that the majority of formerly incarcerated individuals seek employment (93.3% compared with 83.8% of the public) and want a job yet face many economic and social challenges linked to their criminal history, educational attainment, and lack of job-readiness skills (Couloute & Kopf, 2018; Justice Center, The Council for State Governments, 2015). In addition, race and gender influence their economic outcomes; Black women have the highest likelihood of working part time or being unemployed after they exit jail or prison.

Mental Health Disparities

Mental illness is the second major cause of disability across the world (Office of the Surgeon General, 2001; World Health Organization, 2014). Psychiatric disorders, race, and justice involvement are intersecting and compounding factors that increase the psychosocial difficulties and negative outcomes experienced by individuals in the U.S. correctional system. A large proportion of justice-involved youth and adults have at least one diagnosable psychiatric disorder, and the prevalence of mental illness in correctional populations far exceeds the rates in the general public. Compared with White adolescents with externalizing behavior problems (e.g., physical and verbal aggression), a greater percentage of racial and ethnic minority youth with similar concerns are referred to juvenile justice (American Psychiatric Association, 2017). People of color with psychiatric disorders are less likely to receive mental health care both in the community and in the correctional system (Kaba et al., 2015; Pope, 2019; Youman et al., 2010). Scholars estimate that 8% of court-involved, nonincarcerated youth with psychiatric disorders receive mental health or substance use services (Tolou-Shams et al., 2019). About 5% of offenders with substance use problems are admitted to drug treatment courts; 6% to 10% of inmates and 17% of probationers participate in therapeutic programming behind bars and in the community (Belenko et al., 2013). In many cases, untreated mental illness increases a person's risk for technical violations that result in suspended or revoked probation or parole, increased lengths of stay behind bars, and even solitary confinement (Osher et al., 2012).

Severe Mental Illness

An estimated 7% of parolees and 9% of probationers had a severe mental disorder (Osher et al., 2012), and up to one quarter of individuals in jails and prisons (14%–26%) experienced serious psychological distress, compared with 5% in the general U.S. population (Bronson & Berzofsky, 2017). Female inmates had higher rates of severe mental disorders than males (20%–32% vs. 14%–26%) and were about 3 times more likely to have any type of mental health diagnosis (Bronson & Berzofsky, 2017; Osher et al., 2012). Among incarcerated populations, the most common mental illnesses were major depressive disorder (up to one third) and bipolar disorder (up to one quarter; Bronson & Berzofsky, 2017). A greater percentage of inmates with severe mental illness received sanctions for verbal or physical assault during detention (14% compared with 4% of individuals without a diagnosis; Bronson & Berzofsky, 2017).

Likewise, 50% to 75% of justice-involved youth experience mental illness, compared with 8% in the general population (Federal Interagency Forum on Child and Family Statistics, 2019; Justice Center, The Council of State Governments, 2015; Office of Juvenile Justice and Delinquency Prevention, 2017a; Schubert & Mulvey, 2014). Research suggests that the majority of juveniles who enter detention facilities meet the criteria for a psychiatric disorder other than disruptive behavior problems (57% and 58% for African American male and female youth, respectively; 62% and 68% for the Hispanic groups; and 72% and 67% for the non-Hispanic White groups; Teplin et al., 2015). Of those youth with at least one mental health diagnosis, 39% have co-occurring disorders (Schubert & Mulvey, 2014). Anxiety and mood disorders are more prevalent among girls, and disruptive behaviors are 2 to 3 times more likely in boys compared with girls.

Disabilities

Among justice-involved youth, the prevalence of disabilities is almost 4 times as high as in the general population (46% compared with 8%–12%; Grigorenko et al., 2019). Learning disabilities and emotional disturbances are the most frequent and co-occurring disorders, with rates that range from 18% to 42% (Grigorenko et al., 2019). A disproportionate number of racial and ethnic minority youth with disabilities are involved in the U.S. juvenile justice system, and the number of adjudications among justice-involved youth with a learning disability is 220% higher than that for other peers (Grigorenko et al., 2019; OJJDP, 2017a).

About two thirds of justice-involved youth have also had some contact with the child welfare system (Zajac et al., 2013). These so-called dual-status youth typically have a history of child maltreatment (i.e., abuse, neglect), were exposed to domestic violence, or both (Herz et al., 2012). Most of them are members of a racial and ethnic community and have special education needs as well as school, mental health, and substance use problems; they engage in delinquency at a younger age and commit more violent crimes than other juvenile offenders (Herz et al., 2012). About 40% of dual-status youth are girls (Federal Interagency Forum on Child and Family Statistics, 2019); they are more likely than boys to have experienced sexual victimization (Grayson, 2014). The recidivism rates of adolescents with a history of justice and child welfare involvement are 2 to 3 times higher than those of other juvenile offenders (Federal Interagency Forum on Child and Family Statistics, 2019).

Trauma

Family violence and child maltreatment are common traumatic stressors reported by youths and adults in juvenile and criminal justice settings (Ford et al., 2013). Other forms of adversity include exposure to community violence (e.g., witnessing someone being shot, learning about the violent death of a relative), traumatic loss (e.g., extended separation from primary caregivers, multiple out-of-home placements), family difficulties (e.g., incarceration of a family member; family history of mental illness and substance misuse), and intimate partner violence (Dierkhising et al., 2013; Vitopoulos et al., 2019).

According to a study conducted by the Centers for Disease Control and Prevention (CDC) and Kaiser Permanente (CDC, 2020), adverse childhood experiences (ACEs) are prevalent in the general population: Two thirds of the study participants (62%) reported one or more traumatic stressors, child maltreatment, and/or family challenges, including parental separation or divorce and exposure to domestic violence. About one in four (23.5%) had experienced one ACE, and one in six (15.8%) had experienced four or more (CDC, 2020). By comparison, research on juvenile offenders indicates that the prevalence of childhood trauma in the juvenile justice population is 3 to 4 times higher than in the general public: Up to 90% of justice-involved youth have experienced at least two types of ACEs, and a little over half (52%) have experienced four or more (Baglivio, Epps, et al., 2014).

There are gender differences in the frequency and type of traumatic stress offenders experience in childhood, adolescence, and adulthood as well. Girls are more likely than boys to report at least two forms of childhood maltreatment, with rates ranging from 45% to 92% for female youth and from 26% to 89% for male youth (Baglivio, Epps, et al., 2014; Vitopoulos et al., 2019). On average, girls are exposed to four or more categories of ACEs. They also have higher prevalence rates for each type of traumatic stress. Sex abuse is the most salient gender difference: It is 4 times more common among girls (31%) than boys (7%; Baglivio, Epps, et al., 2014). Family violence, parental separation or divorce, and incarceration of a family member are the most prevalent forms of adversity for both female and male youth in the justice system (between 65% and 84%; Baglivio, Epps, et al., 2014).

Exposure to multiple ACEs, including nonvictimization trauma, such as separation from primary caregivers, is a prominent characteristic of justice-involved populations. It is linked to poor psychosocial outcomes; substance use disorders (SUDs); and posttraumatic stress (PTS) symptoms such as emotion dysregulation, dissociation, impulsivity, reactive aggression, and relational problems across the life cycle (Ford et al., 2013). Estimates indicate that the lifetime prevalence of PTS symptoms is 4 to 8 times higher in the juvenile justice system compared with the community (Ford et al., 2013). Likewise, in the adult correctional population women and men are 5 and 8 times more likely to report PTS symptoms than the general public. The number of female prisoners with a diagnosis of posttraumatic stress disorder is 3 times that of the number of incarcerated men (Baranyi et al., 2018). The evidence suggests there are no gender differences in the proportion of juvenile offenders with PTS symptoms (30% male and 34% female;

Vitopoulos et al., 2019). Research on juvenile offenders has also highlighted a link between traumatic stress, criminal history, anxiety, and conduct and affective problems (Jäggi et al., 2016; Wilson et al., 2013). Among adult prisoners, depression and anxiety are the most frequent comorbid diagnoses with posttraumatic stress disorder (Facer-Irwin et al., 2019). The relation between traumatic stress and substance use is discussed in the next section.

Substance Use

Drug offenses are a prevalent category of crime for adults under correctional supervision. In 2020, the majority of federal prisoners were serving time for a drug offense (45.4%; Federal Bureau of Prisons, 2020). In 2016, drug-related convictions (i.e., driving under the influence and other drug offenses) represented 38% of all individuals on probation (Kaeble, 2018) and 15% of state prisoners (Bronson & Carson, 2019). Women (24.8%–56.8%) were more likely than men (14%–46.6%) to be incarcerated for a drug offense (Bronson & Carson, 2019). According to the National Association of Drug Court Professionals (n.d.), another 140,000 offenders with one or more SUDs are supervised by drug treatment courts in the community. Drug offenses constitute a small share of all delinquency cases; however, their rate has increased dramatically for both female and male youth ages 12 to 17. In late adolescence, they are about 18 to 25 times higher, and boys are more likely than girls, to be charged with a drug offense (14% compared with 12%; Hockenberry & Puzzanchera, 2019).

SUDs coincide with traumatic stress, delinquency, and criminal conduct (Bright et al., 2017; Brown & Shillington, 2017; W. Chen et al., 2011), and are 3.5 to 10 times higher among justice-involved individuals compared with the broader public (Fearn et al., 2016). SUDs are a pervasive concern across all segments of the correctional population, youths and adults, in detention facilities and in the community. In 2012, more than one third of male probationers (40.3%) and parolees (38.3%) ages 18 to 49 met the criteria for alcohol and/or drug use disorders (Substance Abuse and Mental Health Services Administration, 2014). Likewise, about half of women supervised in the community (59% on probation and 46% on parole) reported illicit drug use in the past 2 years (Golder et al., 2014). Alcohol use was more prevalent than illicit drug use among male probationers (29.8%) and parolees (24.9%; Substance Abuse and Mental Health Services Administration, 2014). Drinking was also common among female offenders; however, the use of marijuana was more frequent, followed by cocaine and opiates (Golder et al., 2014). Young male adults ages 18 to 25 years with lower levels of education and income represent the largest proportion of probationers with alcohol and drug use problems (Fearn et al., 2016). Racial differences have also been observed, with non-Hispanic White probationers at greater risk for substance dependence (both alcohol and illicit drugs) than other racial and ethnic groups (Fearn et al., 2016).

A large majority of prisoners (72%) and jail inmates (75%) reported habitual drug use in the period between 2007 and 2009; the prevalence of SUDs ranged from 58% (prison) to 63% (jail) and was 12 to 14 times higher than in the general population (5%; Bronson et al., 2017). Marijuana use (77%–78%) was the most widespread, followed by cocaine and crack (47%–52%), hallucinogens (36%), stimulants (34%), depressants (34%), and heroin and other opiates (28%). More than two thirds of incarcerated offenders (37%–42%) reported they were under the influence of drugs when they committed the offense for which they were serving a sentence; and 1 in 4 indicated that crime was a means to obtain drugs (Bronson et al., 2017; National Institute on Drug Abuse, 2019). Like probationers and parolees, White inmates (42%–47%) had higher rates of regular drug use than other racial and ethnic groups (Bronson et al., 2017). Women prisoners (49%) were more likely than men (41%) to have used drugs at the time of the offense; they were also more likely to report habitual cocaine use (Bronson et al., 2017). In general, female offenders with a history of traumatic experiences (e.g., physical and sexual assault, intimate partner violence) and high levels of distress are vulnerable to SUDs (McKee & Hilton, 2019) and co-occurring mental illness (39%–46% of women in jail; Golder et al., 2015; Lynch et al., 2012).

Research on service utilization in the community shows racial and economic disparities among individuals with SUDs: Dropout rates in alcohol and drug use programs are higher for Blacks, Hispanics, and Native Americans compared with Whites and Asians (Saloner & Lê Cook, 2013). Socioeconomic factors—in particular, unemployment and housing instability—have been found to explain racial differences in treatment completion.

Substance use among justice-involved youth is remarkably high: It may affect up to 90% of juvenile offenders (Baggio et al., 2019). Delinquency researchers report rates of SUDs that range from 35% to 59% and are 3 to 4 times higher than in the general population (Mulvey, Schubert, & Chassin, 2010; Teplin et al., 2015). SUDs are less prevalent among African American juvenile offenders than among their Hispanic and non-Hispanic White peers (Mulvey et al., 2010). Empirical findings also indicate that justice-involved youth use multiple substances, with marijuana (85%) and alcohol (80%) being the most common, followed by hallucinogens (25%) and cocaine (23%; Mulvey et al., 2010). SUDs in juveniles have been linked to persistent offending and poor educational and vocational outcomes (Mulvey et al., 2010; Sickmund & Puzzanchera, 2014). They also are associated with victimization in childhood and adolescence (Bright et al., 2017; Sanders et al., 2018).

IMPLICATIONS FOR CLINICAL PRACTICE

The data presented in this chapter reveal the intersection of diversity factors—racial, gender, socioeconomic—in relation to mental health disparities. They also highlight the psychosocial needs that increase individuals' vulnerability to justice involvement. Educational, racial, and economic disadvantages; neighborhood and family adversity; PTS; mental illness; disabilities; and substance use are salient aspects of everyday life among juvenile and adult offenders. They constitute significant challenges that interactions with the justice system often exacerbate by creating additional burdens and barriers to psychological, relational, social, and economic well-being. Justice involvement places new demands on the person and the family, such as court fees, transportation, and requirements to participate in mental health or addiction treatment. Combined with other factors, these demands may exceed the resources of individuals and their social support networks.

For Sam, Sara, Gabriel, and Julia, the family described at the beginning of this chapter, exposure to violence, substance use, psychiatric disorders, and other disabilities converge with familial and social stressors (e.g., family negativity, economic difficulties, racial discrimination in the family of origin and the community) as well as adverse events (e.g., incarceration and expulsion from school) to increase their vulnerability to negative outcomes. A contextual assessment of the family will explore environmental conditions and consider the effects of poverty, violence, and racism, before formulating a diagnosis, conceptualizing the problem, and selecting interventions (see Chapter 4). It will be important not only to acknowledge the presence of stressors or risks but also to appreciate the strengths, abilities, and processes the family uses to navigate challenges; adapt their functioning; and interact with their environment, social groups, and institutions. Despite significant stressors, the family has continued to provide for each individual's basic needs (e.g., food, shelter); to show support and commitment (e.g., by visiting Sam in jail every week); and to maintain connections, even if conflictual, with each other and with members of their extended family and church. Although their mental health and criminal history highlights clinical problems and needs that may call for specific interventions, such as addiction and trauma-focused treatment, their family history suggests a capacity for growth that is key to clinical practice with correctional populations. Last, a contextual assessment of the family will highlight areas for advocacy interventions, specifically, activities that address social justice issues and their effects on the family's well-being. These may include identifying community-based organizations that provide socially just services to support returning citizens and their families. They may also involve exploring and unlearning negative messages about race, poverty, and gender during treatment (Ratts et al., 2016; Singh et al., 2020). Sam, Sara, Gabriel, and Julia are an interracial family. A clinician could inquire about their racial context with an attitude of humility and ask questions about their experience of racial attributions and privilege in everyday life (e.g., what are the negative effects of discriminatory messages on their well-being?). Chapter 4 elaborates on the concept of cultural humility in treatment and describe how mental health practitioners can address racial, ethnic, and other social differences in the therapeutic relationship.

In the risk–need–responsivity model discussed in Chapter 1, substance abuse is an individual risk factor that increases the odds of reoffending. Chapter 3 expands on the concept of risk and vulnerability and describes the protective processes that influence the behavioral, relational, and social outcomes of justice-involved juveniles and adults. It discusses empirical knowledge about the correlates of delinquency and crime and shows how to incorporate this knowledge in the conceptualization of the fictitious family. It also reviews studies of the relational dynamics that develop around serious mental illness, delinquency, and substance abuse. These dynamics can negatively influence couple and family functioning. In the risk–need–responsivity model, they represent a moderate risk for recidivism. Relationship research on psychopathology gives insight into the couple and family processes that contribute to undesirable outcomes and that are an important focus of therapeutic interventions to enhance the resilience of relational systems.

3 THE ECOLOGY OF DELINQUENCY AND CRIME

Offending and justice involvement are the result of complex direct and indirect relationships among various intrapersonal, relational, and environmental factors. Research in psychology and criminology has begun to uncover the relationships or mechanisms that participate in the development, persistence, and prevention of antisocial conduct among different individuals in diverse contexts. This chapter summarizes current empirical knowledge about the predictors of delinquency and crime and the pathways that link those predictors to lawbreaking behaviors. This knowledge, although emerging and incomplete, is critical to clinical assessment, decision making, and treatment planning. It points at specific areas of intervention, in particular, the risk factors that are linked to higher odds of offending and the processes that protect individuals and families from adverse outcomes.

KEY TERMS AND CONCEPTS

Research on delinquency and crime aims to identify intra- and interindividual variations that explain lawbreaking behaviors. In general, it consists of cross-sectional and longitudinal studies investigating the risk, promotive, and

https://doi.org/10.1037/0000285-004
Best Clinical Practices for Treating Families in Juvenile and Criminal Justice Systems, by C. C. Datchi

protective factors that differentiate offenders from the general public. The concept of "risk factor" originates from the field of public health, where it serves to explain the occurrence of diseases at the individual level (Farrington et al., 2016). In criminology, the term *risk factor* describes variables that increase the odds of offending (Farrington & Welsh, 2006). It is used in conjunction with the terms *promotive factors* and *protective factors*, which refer to conditions that lower the probability of criminal conduct and that moderate or cancel out the impact of risk factors, respectively (Jolliffe et al., 2016; also see Chapter 1, this volume, for a discussion of risk factors in the psychology of criminal conduct).

Risk factors are covariates rather than causes of delinquency and crime. To date, cross-sectional and longitudinal studies have illuminated some of the traits and circumstances that influence an individual's participation in criminal activities, and criminological and psychological theories have described the possible mechanisms by which these variables or risk factors affect behaviors. The principles of *systemic thinking* (see Chapter 1) focus attention on the processes that take place at the interface between the person and the environment, in particular, the within-family transactions wherein individual behaviors are embedded. These transactions develop from family members' reciprocal actions into enduring patterns of relating that act as mediators of behavioral outcomes (Sexton, 2011). For example, childhood disruptive behaviors often occur in the context of parent–child conflict that involves developmentally inappropriate parental expectations, parental negativity in emotions and attribution style, inconsistent discipline, and poor supervision (Beach et al., 2006). The mutual transactions that characterize parent–child conflict (e.g., child noncompliance ←→ parental negativity) contribute to the maintenance of the child's problematic conduct. Research on relational processes and psychopathology also suggests that family dynamics participate in the onset of clinical problems (McFarlane & Cook, 2007). High levels of family-expressed emotions (i.e., criticism, emotional negativity, and overinvolvement) constitute a chronic stressor that activates the predisposing biological factors of severe mental disorders such as psychosis. In this chapter, the principles of family systems theory provide a framework for organizing and understanding empirical knowledge about the predictors of delinquency and crime. To conduct a systemic assessment and gather data that will be useful to case conceptualization and treatment formulation, clinicians must be familiar with the individual, relational, and contextual factors that are linked to the presenting problem; they must also discern how these factors interact and identify leverage points or places where intervention will produce small changes with far-reaching effects on individual behaviors (Stanton & Welsh, 2011).

INDIVIDUAL PREDICTORS OF DELINQUENCY AND CRIME

Research on the correlates of delinquency and crime highlights four intrapersonal variables that influence the course of antisocial behaviors: (a) age; (b) psychological and personality traits, including cognitive abilities; (c) substance use; and (d) trauma. The sections that follow summarize current empirical knowledge about each of these individual factors and their relation to recidivism. When available, findings that describe interactions among and between individual factors and other contextual variables to explain criminal conduct are reported.

Age

In general, there is a curvilinear relationship between age and criminal behaviors: The rates of offending tend to increase in late childhood, hit their highest points between ages 17 and 19, and begin to fall at ages 20 to 29 (Loeber et al., 2014). In 2017, 79% of justice-involved youth were age 10 to 15, 12% were age 16, and 9% were age 17 (Hockenberry & Puzzanchera, 2019). (These numbers do not include older juveniles whose delinquency cases have been waived to criminal courts.) Researchers estimate that 40% to 60% of juvenile offenders stop engaging in criminal activities by the time they reach young adulthood (Loeber et al., 2014). For the minority of youth who develop persistent patterns of antisocial behavior, the transition from adolescence to young adulthood corresponds to an increase in crime severity and violence (e.g., homicide, drug dealing; Loeber et al., 2014). Research suggests that case processing in adult justice systems may produce undesirable outcomes for young adults ages 18 to 20 (Loeber et al., 2014). The negative effects result from the use of harsher punishment in criminal justice compared with juvenile justice systems. This includes longer incarceration sentences that do not take into account the developmental trajectories of crime in adolescence and young adulthood or the fact that most young adults ages 18 to 20 will desist on their own within the next few years (Kim & Peterson, 2014).

Life-course-persistent (LCP) offenders are those with a lasting pattern of antisocial behaviors that develop in early adolescence and continue into adulthood (Jolliffe, Farrington, Piquero, McLeod, & van de Weijer, 2017). They typically are male (nine in 10) with a criminal history that started before age 12 (e.g., stealing, aggression toward other children; Brown et al., 2019). Longitudinal studies suggest that male LCP offenders represent 3% to 13.5% of the general population and have a criminal career that lasts 19 to 30 years (Jolliffe, Farrington, Piquero, McLeod, & van de Weijer, 2017). The prevalence rates of female LCP offenders are relatively small (1.3%–1.6%); most female offenders engage in illegal activities during adolescence up to age 20 (Jolliffe, Farrington, Piquero, McLeod, & van de Weijer, 2017).

Psychological and Personality Traits

Impulsiveness, hyperactivity, risk taking, sensation seeking, poor self-concept and self-esteem, negative attitudes towards the law, low emotional and cognitive empathy, and neuropsychological deficits in cognitive ability and attention are intrapersonal characteristics that increase the odds of offending (Farrington & Welsh, 2006). Low verbal IQ, high hyperactivity and impulsiveness, risk taking, and poor concentration are important childhood risk factors for violence in adolescence and adulthood, ages 10 to 61 (Farrington, 2019; Farrington & Welsh, 2006). These traits may have an enduring effect on individual behaviors: Restlessness and poor attention at age 3 were found to predict self-reported delinquency at ages 18 to 21 (Farrington & Welsh, 2006). Impulsiveness typically decreases as adolescents grow and develop the capacity for self-control (Loeber et al., 2014). Self-control is the product of both genetic and nonshared environmental factors; scholars estimate that heredity explains 45% of the variance in self-control among juvenile delinquents and 36% of the variance in aggressive antisocial behaviors for LCP offenders (Azeredo et al., 2019). Research also suggests that genetic factors have a greater influence on male youth's antisocial behaviors compared with female youth (Azeredo et al., 2019). Last, negative emotions (i.e., anger, irritability) have been linked to recidivism (Hein et al., 2017); both emotional lability and low anxiety may differentiate LCP and adolescence-limited offenders from the general public (Jolliffe, Farrington, Piquero, Loeber, & Hill, 2017), and early pubertal maturation may increase girls' risk for delinquency through their relationships with older partners and risky sexual behaviors (Leve et al., 2015).

Recent studies have investigated the relation of intelligence and educational attainment to delinquency, violence, and recidivism (Farrington, 2019; Farrington & Welsh, 2006; Jolliffe, Farrington, Loeber, & Pardini, 2016; Jolliffe, Farrington, Piquero, McLeod, & van de Weijer, 2017; Kennedy et al., 2019; Savolainen et al., 2018). They yielded evidence that low IQ and poor school performance were independent predictors of aggression and offending in adolescence and adulthood after controlling for other covariates, such as family income and family size (Farrington, 2019; Farrington & Welsh, 2006; Savolainen et al., 2018). Socioeconomic status (SES) moderated the association between IQ and violence, and boys from lower socioeconomic classes were more likely to commit violent crimes (Farrington & Welsh, 2006). Together with low educational attainment, neurocognitive impairments may also be a distinguishing characteristic of chronic offenders (Farrington & Welsh, 2006). Poor academic performance was found to predict the number of arrests among youth with low reading ability who repeated at least one grade (Kennedy et al., 2019). To explain the link between intelligence and criminal conduct, researchers have proposed theories that highlight the negative effects of cognitive deficits on planning, decision making, and empathy, as well as academic functioning (Farrington & Welsh, 2006; Kennedy et al., 2019). Absent appropriate assessment and intervention in childhood and adolescence, low cognitive abilities place students at risk for poor academic achievement, school dropout, rejection by prosocial peers, and antisocial behaviors.

The same variables that predict offending may also decrease the likelihood of criminal conduct; they exist on a continuum where low or high levels of the individual characteristic constitute a protective factor. For example, high empathy is negatively related to delinquency and crime (Farrington & Welsh, 2006). Likewise, high academic achievement and low hyperactivity were found to reduce by 10% the odds of violent behaviors among youth in economically disadvantaged neighborhoods (Jolliffe et al., 2016). School performance interacted with poverty and family characteristics, such that the rates of violent crimes were substantially lower for boys in more deprived and disrupted families than for boys from intact and more privileged backgrounds (Jolliffe et al., 2016). Other individual factors that decrease the likelihood of delinquency and violence include agreeableness, conscientiousness, high shyness, ability to foresee consequences, a positive attitude toward school, depression, and anxiety (Farrington & Welsh, 2006; Hein et al., 2017; Jolliffe et al., 2016).

Substance Use

As discussed in Chapter 2, substance use and offending often coexist (Mulvey et al., 2010). Substance use is a consistent predictor of concurrent and future juvenile recidivism (Kennedy et al., 2019; Mulvey et al., 2010). It also shares common risk factors with delinquency (Curcio et al., 2013). For example, impulsivity, sensation seeking, association with antisocial peers, and weak attachment to school and parental figures have been linked to both problem drinking and offending. Likewise, parental substance use, poor parenting, and family conflict are associated with both juvenile substance use and delinquency (Mulvey et al., 2010). Research indicates that substance use disorders predict shorter times to recidivism for justice-involved youth and women prisoners (C. K. Scott et al., 2016; Wylie & Rufino, 2018). Kopak and Hoffmann (2014) investigated the relation between substance use disorders and offending in a sample of male adult offenders; their findings highlighted the mediating effects of symptom severity on the type of offense; specifically, the more drug dependence symptoms, the greater the likelihood of being charged with a substance-related and nonviolent offense (e.g., drug possession, property) compared with a violent crime. The more symptoms of alcohol dependence, the greater the odds of being arrested for a violent crime (e.g., intimate partner violence, assault). There is also evidence that substance use disorders are associated with exposure to traumatic events for women and that victimization increases the likelihood of reoffending by about one third (C. K. Scott et al., 2016).

The relation between substance use and offending may be bidirectional, whereby substance use increases the likelihood of delinquency and crime, and vice versa (Mulvey et al., 2010). Alcohol and drugs lower inhibitions, thus facilitating participation in illegal activities; criminal behaviors may also be a means to obtain substances (Kopak & Hoffmann, 2014). Substance use may also interfere with youth's cognitive, emotional, and social development in ways that increase their risk for offending in adolescence and adulthood. Alternatively, substance use and offending may be externalizing behavior symptoms that are connected by common risk factors, as mentioned earlier; their development simultaneously or not may depend on the complex interactions between shared factors and other intrapersonal, relational, and contextual variables such as peer influence.

Trauma

The relation between trauma and lawbreaking behaviors has received much empirical attention. There is some evidence that trauma may influence youth's decisions to engage in delinquent behaviors (Solomon et al., 2012). Together, victimization and exposure to stressful life events predicted violent offenses by adolescent males (Maschi, 2006). Studies have found an indirect link between girls' and women's victimization and offending (Kruttschnitt et al., 2019; Wylie & Rufino, 2018): Childhood and adult maltreatment (e.g., childhood physical abuse, intimate partner violence in adulthood) increases girls' and women's risk of poor mental health outcomes (e.g., serious mental illness), which in turn increase the odds of committing a crime (DeHart et al., 2014; Karatzias et al., 2018; Lynch et al., 2013).

Scientific findings also suggest there is a positive relation between the number of adverse experiences and the severity of offending (Karatzias et al.,

2018) and between specific types of victimization and crime, for example, between caregiver violence and girls' running away in adolescence and between intimate partner violence and commercial sex work and drug dealing in adulthood (Lynch et al., 2013). Among female and male youth ages 13 to 19 involved in the child welfare system, repeated victimization increased the odds of entering the juvenile justice system at younger ages by 60% to 102% (Cho et al., 2019; Vitopoulos et al., 2019). Child sex abuse was associated with recidivism for female juvenile offenders, but not for male youth; the risk was 5 times higher for justice-involved girls with a history of sexual victimization compared with female peers who had not experienced child sex abuse (Conrad et al., 2014). Trauma may also have a lasting impact on girls' and women's criminal trajectories: Exposure to family violence in childhood was found to increase the risk of arrest in adulthood for justice-involved girls, but not for boys (Rhoades et al., 2016). In sum, the research findings indicate it is important to consider typical delinquent behaviors such as running away, aggression, risky sexual behaviors, and substance use in the context of youth's trauma history: These behaviors may be symptoms of complex posttraumatic stress rather than indicators of antisocial traits. When left unaddressed, complex posttraumatic stress may explain the persistence of offending in adolescence and adulthood.

Emotion regulation is one of the hypothesized psychological mechanisms that link trauma to delinquency and crime. Scholars posit that adverse experiences interfere with the development of emotion regulation and thus reduce a person's capacity for self-control, which is an important predictor of aggressive behaviors (Maschi, 2006; Theobald et al., 2013). Attachment theory calls attention to the role of relational environments in self-regulation. In particular, children's biologically based bond to adult caregivers, or *attachment figures*, is theorized to influence the formation of internal working models or schemas of self and others (Johnson, 2003). These schemas are templates for forming relationships; they also function as a lens that influences meaning making as well as affective and interpersonal self-regulation in ways that determine individuals' response to adverse experiences and their risk for delinquency and crime (Amatya & Barzman, 2012). Likewise, feminist theories emphasize the role of violence exposure and relationships with family and significant others in the onset and persistence of girls' and women's offending (Blanchette & Brown, 2019). The *pathways theory*, which has received some empirical support, suggests that experiences of interpersonal violence in childhood and adulthood may result in the development of psychiatric symptoms and comorbid substance use that increase girls' and women's risk of justice involvement (Gehring, 2018). Recent evidence linking victimization to overall risk of recidivism and criminogenic needs in the family domain also suggests that it is important to consider the relation among delinquency, criminal conduct, and couple and family dynamics (Vitopoulos et al., 2019).

RELATIONSHIP FACTORS LINKED TO DELINQUENCY AND CRIME

Relationship science has described the interpersonal processes that influence the onset and the course of clinical problems (see Beach et al., 2006). This section discusses current knowledge of familial and couple dynamics that have been linked to delinquency and crime. The information pertains to the relational domain of systemic assessment in clinical practice with couples and families.

The Family Environment

The family is a primary site of influence on youth development, and several family characteristics have been linked to juvenile delinquency. Parenting practices, the quality of the parent–child bond, parental stress, family conflict and violence, family communication, and family cohesion are the main factors most often cited in the empirical literature (Azeredo et al., 2019; P. Chen et al., 2016; Farrington, 2019; Jolliffe et al., 2016; Jolliffe, Farrington, Piquero, Loeber, & Hill, 2017; Kennedy et al., 2019; Leve et al., 2015). Studies have also investigated the effects of family structure and family resources, including separation and divorce, a single-parent household, family size, parent work schedules, and socioeconomic status (Evans et al., 2016; Hendrix & Parcel, 2014; Jolliffe et al., 2016; Jolliffe, Farrington, Piquero, Loeber, & Hill, 2017; Kwong Wong, 2017; Li, 2014; Mack et al., 2007; Theobald et al., 2013; VanderPyl, 2018).

Parenting

With regard to parenting, supervision, discipline, and parental involvement in childhood and adolescence are strong predictors of offending (Farrington, 2019; Jolliffe et al., 2016; Kennedy et al., 2019; Sickmund & Puzzanchera, 2014). Harsh discipline, low parental monitoring, and lack of parental involvement are risk factors that increase the likelihood of juvenile delinquency. Evidence suggests they also are associated with violence convictions in adulthood (Farrington, 2019). By contrast, high levels of parental supervision, developmentally appropriate parenting, and positive parental involvement act as protective factors against delinquency; in particular, they were found to reduce violence by 10% among boys who experienced family disruption (Jolliffe et al., 2016). Recent studies also have highlighted the effects of caregivers' psychiatric symptoms and family religiosity on parenting and delinquency (Folk et al., 2020; Li, 2014; Tolou-Shams et al., 2018). Severe mental illness has been linked to lower levels of parental monitoring and caregivers' report of poor family functioning, including low family cohesion and communication (Folk et al., 2020; Tolou-Shams et al., 2018). Poor monitoring and family functioning combined may increase the risk of juvenile offending. Li (2014) found that *familial religiosity*, or participation in religious activities, had a positive direct effect on parental supervision, involvement, and positive reinforcement and a negative indirect effect on delinquency. Recent studies have found an indirect positive association between parenting stress and juvenile offending (Lucero et al., 2015; Voisin, Kim, Bassett, & Marotta, 2020). Higher self-esteem protects youth from the negative effects of parental stress; together with youth's future orientation or ability to set future goals and plans, it also mediated the relation between parental stress and delinquency (Voisin et al., 2020).

Family Dynamics

The term *family dynamics* here refers to family communication, family cohesion, and family conflict. These factors were found to discriminate LCP offenders from their adolescence-limited counterparts, and poor parental communication was one of the strongest predictors of chronic offending (Jolliffe, Farrington, Piquero, McLeod, & van de Weijer, 2017). Meldrum and colleagues (2016) investigated the links among parental self-control, family cohesion, family conflict, and delinquency; their results provided additional evidence that family dynamics mediated the effects of caregivers' individual characteristics on juvenile offending. To be specific, low parental self-control had an indirect influence on youth's antisocial behaviors through its positive association with family conflict (a risk factor) and negative association with family cohesion (a protective factor). Likewise, Mowen and Boman (2018) evaluated the effects of family conflict on juvenile delinquency before and after incarceration. Their findings showed a positive relation between pre- and postincarceration levels of family conflict. They also suggested that family conflict decreased over time when the family communicated support, that elevated family conflict was linked to increased association with antisocial peers after release, and that both family conflict and delinquent peers predicted the severity of offending and substance use after incarceration. Taylor and Borduin (2014) examined whether there were gender differences in parent–child, verbal aggression, and nonverbal aggression in a sample of juvenile offenders and nonoffenders. Their results indicated higher rates of relational aggression between justice-involved female youth and their mothers compared with other groups. These findings suggest that family dynamics, and mother–child conflict in particular, are important to consider in the treatment of justice-involved girls.

Parent–Child Bond

The quality of the parent–child bond is a significant predictor of behavioral outcomes in childhood and adolescence. Youth who have a warm and supportive relationship with their parents tend to succeed at school and show prosocial tendencies (Cavanagh & Cauffman, 2017). Cavanagh and Cauffman (2017) found that maternal warmth, in particular, had a protective effect for first-time male offenders ages 13 to 17: Youth who experienced higher levels of maternal warmth before their first contact with the justice system were more likely to commit low-level offenses and less likely to recidivate. Likewise, Brown and Shillington (2017) reported a main effect of protective adult relationships on juvenile delinquency: Youth in the child welfare system who identified the presence of supportive and reliable adults were less likely to engage in antisocial behaviors. Lippold and colleagues (2018) studied the effects of change in parental warmth and hostility from childhood to early adolescence; their results suggested that higher fluctuations in father's warmth and parental hostility, as perceived by youth, were associated with greater delinquency in ninth grade for girls only (Lippold et al., 2018). The empirical literature reports that youth who have weak attachment bonds to their parents are at greater risk for offending (Azeredo et al., 2019; Curcio et al., 2013; Fagan et al., 2011).

Family Structure

Parental separation and divorce typically result in family disruptions and changes in family structure and caregiving. They represent challenging transitions in the family life cycle. In the presence of other conditions, they can also constitute a risk factor for criminal conduct (Azeredo et al., 2019). For example, family disruption in childhood has been linked to juvenile delinquency and violent offenses in adulthood (Farrington, 2019; Krohn et al., 2009; Theobald et al., 2013). Caregiver transitions were found to increase the odds that justice-involved adolescent girls would engage in acts of delinquency (Leve et al., 2015). Research suggests that a family breakdown has an indirect effect on offending that is mediated by parental supervision and child discipline (Theobald et al., 2013). Poor parental supervision is a covariate of family disruption: Being divorced and single can reduce parents' ability to monitor children's activities, which in turn may have adverse effects on adolescents' behaviors. Likewise, a family breakdown, when combined with harsh discipline, is a predictor of criminal conduct in adulthood. In other words, it is the interaction between family structure and relational processes, rather than family structure alone, that influences the odds of delinquency and crime (Hendrix & Parcel, 2014; Theobald et al., 2013). Research on single-parent families, parent work schedules, fathering, and delinquency offers additional insight into the importance of family relationship quality. In a sample of male juvenile offenders ages 13 to 17, youth who enjoyed a warm father–child relationship characterized by low hostility had lower delinquency rates than peers with absent and harsh fathers, and those with absent fathers were less likely to engage in antisocial behaviors than adolescents with harsh fathers, after controlling for the quality of the mother–child relationship (Simmons et al., 2018). Family bonding was found to reduce the negative impact of parental unemployment and nonstandard work schedule on juvenile delinquency (Hendrix & Parcel, 2014). A longitudinal study that compared the effects of relationship quality and father's presence found no significant association between father involvement and delinquency; however, the results showed that higher levels of trust and communication in the father–child relationship were linked to greater reductions in delinquent behaviors over time (Yoder et al., 2016). Likewise, studies have investigated the effects of single-parent households and produced evidence that family structure did not have a direct effect on youth externalizing behavior problems; however, youth who reported strong maternal attachment bonds presented lower levels of risk for nonsevere delinquency, and vice versa (Mack et al., 2007).

Mothers represent the majority of single-parent households in the United States (VanderPyl, 2018). Single adolescent mothers in particular experience significant challenges that increase their children's risk for justice involvement, such as lower income levels and larger family size (Jolliffe et al., 2016). Mothers' age at first childbirth was found to predict male youth's persistence in offending (van Vugt et al., 2016); the effect of maternal age was partially explained by elevated levels of parenting stress, high numbers of children, and negative parent–child communication.

Marital and Intimate Partner Relationships

Substantial evidence exists that marriage and cohabitation have a prosocial effect on adult offenders, men in particular (Abeling-Judge, 2016; Bersani

& Doherty, 2013; Doherty & Bersani, 2016; Doherty & Ensminger, 2013; Larson et al., 2016; Lyngstad & Skardhamar, 2013; Rocque et al., 2015; Sampson et al., 2006). Researchers theorize that marriage and cohabitation facilitate the development of relational systems in which individuals assume specific roles and responsibilities and establish routines for everyday life that limit opportunities for leisure activities and interactions with peers (Sampson et al., 2006). In addition, scholars posit that couple relationships are attachment bonds that connect people to each other and to conventional institutions: The stronger the bond, the more the person invests in the institutions of marriage and family, and the lower the likelihood of offending (Bersani & Doherty, 2013). Couple and family relationships may also represent informal sources of supervision and accountability that protect individuals from antisocial influence.

Several studies have reported that being married and being in a cohabiting relationship are associated with reductions in arrest and recidivism that range from 25% to 45% (Bersani & Doherty, 2013; Doherty & Ensminger, 2013; Sampson et al., 2006). The results indicate that the effects of marriage were significant for various types of crime, including substance-related, property, and violent offenses (Sampson et al., 2006). They also highlight similar patterns of desistance across racial groups, but not across gender. Doherty and Ensminger (2013) found that married Black women experienced a 10% decrease in arrest for property offenses only; unlike their male counterparts, their marital status increased the likelihood of drug-related arrest and did not have a significant impact on violent crime. This finding points to the influence of romantic relationships on women's criminal trajectories: Intimate partners and family members are often involved in women's introduction to drug use and initiation into crime (Kreis et al., 2016). Women tend to follow intersecting pathways that lead to substance-related problems and offending: Adverse experiences and dysfunctional parenting in childhood increase women's vulnerability to interpersonal abuse in adulthood; they also increase the odds of forming violent relationships with drug-using and antisocial partners that will support addiction and crime (Kreis et al., 2016). Evidence also indicates that spouses may have an influence on male offending and that men who are married to a criminal or deviant partner are more likely to recidivate (Sampson et al., 2006).

Researchers have investigated the effects of relationship dissolution on criminal conduct and shown that divorce is associated with an average 52% increase in arrest rates for both men and women who were married for 2 years or more (Bersani & Doherty, 2013). In a sample of Black men, divorce was associated with a 34% and 44% increase in violent and property offenses, respectively (Doherty & Bersani, 2016). Legal separation had a significant impact on women only. Justice-involved youth were found to engage in more acts of delinquency in the period that followed the breakup of their own romantic relationships (Larson et al., 2016). In young adulthood, levels of reoffending were higher after the dissolution of cohabiting relationships compared with dating relationships; the effects of cohabitation on criminal behaviors were mediated by peer influence (Larson et al., 2016). Stable cohabiting relationships appeared to protect individuals from the impact of antisocial associates; similarly, neighborhood characteristics emerged as a potential moderating factor. Doherty and Bersani (2016) found that Black male offenders who resided in more advantaged communities by young adulthood were less likely to recidivate after divorce; their social and economic conditions (e.g., higher income levels, greater involvement in community organizations) supported their progress toward a prosocial lifestyle.

In sum, the research on intimate relationships and crime highlights the interpersonal processes that are involved in the reduction of criminal conduct. When couple and family relationships are defined by mutual support and a sense of togetherness and interdependency, and when they offer opportunities to take on prosocial roles and identities, they are influential in preventing and reducing antisocial behaviors (Datchi, 2017a; Weaver & McNeill, 2015).

CONTEXTUAL FACTORS LINKED TO DELINQUENCY AND CRIME

From a bioecological and systemic perspective, criminal conduct is viewed as the outcome of reciprocal influences among interacting factors: individual traits and relational factors (i.e., family and peer), as well as environmental conditions in proximal settings, such as the neighborhood (Ferguson & Evans, 2019). Neighborhood conditions include socioeconomic disadvantage (e.g., number of families living below the poverty line and receiving public assistance, percentage of female-headed households), residential instability, community violence, level of collective efficacy, ethnic heterogeneity, and neighborhood integration. *Collective efficacy* is a concept that describes the extent to which people participate in the socialization of youth and the prevention of violence in the neighborhood, for example, whether they intervene when they witness an act of delinquency (Kurlychek et al., 2012). *Neighborhood integration* is the network of social bonds between residents, how much they know and talk to each other and how much they trust each other (Kurlychek et al., 2012). *Residential instability* denotes the degree to which individuals and families move in and out of the neighborhood. The following sections describe research findings that explain how neighborhood and peer factors influence offending in adolescence and adulthood. They conclude with a discussion of the impact of justice involvement on delinquent and criminal behaviors.

Neighborhood Factors

Delinquency, violence, and crime rates are typically more elevated in densely populated, disadvantaged urban areas with a lower percentage of owner-occupied houses and greater residential mobility (Farrington & Welsh, 2006; Kennedy et al., 2019). Youth who live in areas of concentrated disadvantage are at greater risk for serious delinquency, as well as for alcohol use, family violence, and child maltreatment (Kennedy et al., 2019; Wolff et al., 2018). They are also more likely to engage in aggressive behaviors and acts of serious violence over longer periods of time, compared with their male counterparts in advantaged communities (Fabio et al., 2011; Jolliffe et al., 2016). In addition, statistics show that high-crime neighborhoods have a large proportion of low-income female-headed families living in poor housing (Farrington & Welsh, 2006). The physical concentration of low-income single-mother families appears to have an effect on juvenile delinquency: At the neighborhood level, the percentage of single-mother families was found to be associated with increases in youth total crime rates (Kwong Wong, 2017).

Housing Instability and Neighborhood Cohesion

Neighborhood research has also investigated the effects of environmental factors on prisoner reentry. Most inmates leave prison to return to disadvantaged communities where they face considerable economic and social challenges: They may have little money and savings; they may not qualify for public housing and government assistance (e.g., the Supplemental Nutrition Assistance Program), and they may have to rely on family and friends for a temporary residence (Mears & Cochran, 2015). Researchers estimate that three quarters of released prisoners live with family members and that up to one quarter are homeless (Mears & Cochran, 2015). Unstable living conditions paired with employment barriers such as limited job skills, no driving license, background checks, and discrimination may increase the risk of recidivism for former prisoners residing in disadvantaged neighborhoods (Morenoff & Harding, 2014).

Although it is difficult to empirically determine the mechanisms that link neighborhood factors and offending, research findings have provided support for the criminological theory of informal social control (Karlidag & Morris, 2019; Kotlaja & Meier, 2019). *Informal social control* refers to the processes whereby communities influence individuals to conform to social norms and values (Kurlychek et al., 2012). It requires networks of kinship and friendship that provide a sense of belonging. These social ties are sparse in communities characterized by family disruption, residential instability, and poor social integration; as a result, residents may be less inclined to intervene to support conformity to a prosocial lifestyle (Kurlychek et al., 2012). Studies have found negative associations between youth conduct problems and measures of neighborhood bonding, neighborhood cohesion, and collective socialization (P. Chen et al., 2016; Kurlychek et al., 2012; Stevens, 2018). They show that collective efficacy is negatively related to juvenile delinquency and association with antisocial peers (Farrington & Welsh, 2006) and that neighborhood factors such as social integration protect individuals from risks in the peer and school domains (Kurlychek et al., 2012). Study results also have confirmed the important role of familial processes, in particular, family warmth and parental monitoring, as protective factors against delinquency for adolescents exposed to community violence (P. Chen et al., 2016; Stevens, 2018).

Macrosystemic Factors

At a broader level, race, gender, poverty, and culture influence individuals' interactions with their proximal environment: the family and the neighborhood. For example, ethnic and racial discrimination was found to interact with community violence to predict conduct problems in a sample of Latino adolescents (Rubens et al., 2018). To be specific, exposure to community violence was associated with delinquent behaviors at low levels of ethnic and racial discrimination. In a sample of Black youth ages 10 to 19, early and increased exposure to racial discrimination was predictive of early-onset, chronic offending (Evans et al., 2016). A qualitative study of community factors linked to juvenile crime also showed that incarcerated youth perceived racism and gender expectations as major social stressors and motivators for breaking the law (Barnert et al., 2015). The youth also described greater levels of ethnic and racial segregation and police presence in the neighborhood and identified poverty as the most influential determinant of delinquency. Low family income, dependence on government financial assistance, and poor-quality housing have consistently been associated with juvenile and adult offending (Farrington & Welsh, 2006; Jolliffe et al., 2016; Leve et al., 2015; Lucero et al., 2015; C. K. Scott et al., 2016; VanderPyl, 2018). Azeredo and colleagues (2019) found a curvilinear relationship between delinquency and family SES and higher rates of youth offending at low and high levels of family SES. Low and colleagues (2012) studied the pathways to delinquency in economically strained and more financially advantaged families and noted that the presence of economic stressors heightened the effects of harsh and inconsistent parenting and the effects of older sibling externalizing behaviors on younger sibling delinquency. The transmission of conduct problems occurred through sibling relational aggression and older sibling association with antisocial peers. Again, the research highlights the role of family processes and their interaction with contextual factors: In particular, it shows that parenting practices and family conflict in the presence of economic stressors mediate the relation between family SES and juvenile delinquency (Farrington & Welsh, 2006).

Peer Affiliation

Affiliation with antisocial others is a major predictor of lawbreaking behaviors in the psychology of criminal conduct (Andrews & Bonta, 2015), and there is strong evidence that associating with deviant peers is related to offending in adolescence and adulthood (Andrews & Bonta, 2015; Evans et al., 2016; Farrington & Welsh, 2006; Henneberger et al., 2014; Jolliffe et al., 2016; Kennedy et al., 2019). For example, boys age 17 and under are more likely to engage in acts of delinquency with other youth (Farrington & Welsh, 2006). Association with delinquent peers is linked to juvenile recidivism (Kennedy et al., 2019); it supports the early onset and persistence of offending from adolescence to early adulthood (Evans et al., 2016; Farrington & Welsh, 2006). The scientific literature describes gender differences in peer influence; in particular, girls' delinquent behaviors appear to be motivated by friendships and romantic relationships with older male youth (Leve et al., 2015). The research also highlights interactions among family dynamics, peer influence, and community factors. In a sample of Black and White adolescent offenders, youths' connection with community and institutional resources (e.g., participation in after-school programs) was related to higher levels of family functioning, and family cohesion and effective parenting were linked to prosocial peer relationships (E. P. Smith et al., 2016). By contrast, problematic family functioning had an indirect effect on delinquency mediated by youths' negative peer affiliation (E. P. Smith et al., 2016). A review of the literature shows that peer influence is stronger when parental monitoring is low, and family bonds moderate the negative impact of peer deviance on adolescent behaviors (Henneberger et al., 2014). The interaction between family dynamics and peer affiliation may start in childhood, with poor parenting practices and family relationships that support aggressive and other antisocial behaviors (Andrews & Bonta, 2015). Conduct problems may limit children's capacity to develop prosocial relationships and, during adolescence, increase the likelihood they will join deviant peer groups that model and reward procriminal behaviors.

Contact With the Justice System

Recidivism rates for justice-involved youth and adults range from 21% for juvenile offenders on probation to 70% for state prisoners (Alarid & Rangel, 2018; C. J. Smith & Young, 2017). On average, 55% of incarcerated youth are rearrested within 1 year of being discharged, and 24% return to confinement (Office of Juvenile Justice and Delinquency Prevention, 2017b). Reincarceration rates for state prisoners and jail inmates are as high as 50% to 60% (Comfort, 2016; C. J. Smith & Young, 2017). These elevated numbers have raised questions about the effects of justice contact; research has shown that justice involvement is associated with a variety of adverse outcomes not only for individuals who have been adjudicated or convicted of a crime but also for those close to them (Comfort et al., 2016).

Impact on Juvenile Outcomes

Contact with the justice system was found to increase violent offending for youth who received the most punitive sentence (i.e., adjudication; Beardslee et al., 2019). There was no change in delinquent behavior for adolescents with no justice involvement, and youth who were dismissed or diverted to probation and other treatment programs reported a decrease in violent, theft, and property crimes (Beardslee et al., 2019). The odds of being rearrested were higher for all justice-involved juvenile offenders, however, regardless of the severity of their sentence. This suggests that justice system contact increases adolescents' risk of becoming entangled with it. Lack of family resources may compound the problem: The caregivers of justice-involved youth experience many challenges (e.g., child care, economic hardship, lack of transportation, language barriers) that can prevent them from satisfying the conditions set forth by the court (e.g., mental health counseling, program fees; Amani et al., 2018). As a result, youth may not be discharged from legal supervision until they have met all the requirements.

Impact on Couple and Family Relationships

Justice involvement, and incarceration in particular, puts new pressures on the families of juvenile and adult offenders: separation, loss, and reconfiguration of family roles and responsibilities; relational conflict; costs associated with correctional supervision, therapy, and transportation to the treatment or detention facility; loss of wages for taking time off to visit relatives behind bars; eviction and residential instability; parenting stress; poorer health; and social stigma are some of the indirect effects that families experience as a result of justice contact (Aaron & Dallaire, 2010; Comfort et al., 2016; Datchi et al., 2016; Turney & Goodsell, 2018; VanderPyl, 2018). They represent a form of adversity that can reduce or prevent family support and involvement in offender rehabilitation. In turn, reduced family support and involvement may have a negative impact on offenders' outcomes. In a sample of incarcerated youth, the frequency of family visitation during confinement was negatively related to the number of adolescent problem behaviors per month; youth who received infrequent, or no, family visits displayed more disruptive behaviors and had lower grade point average compared with their peers who received regular family visits (Villalobos Agudelo, 2013). Likewise, incarceration was found to create instability in cohabiting and marital relationships: It was associated with high levels of couple conflict as well as high probabilities of separation, divorce, and living alone after release (Apel, 2016; Turney & Goodsell, 2018). Instability in relationship status persisted for up to 5 years after release (Apel, 2016). Given that stable cohabiting and marital relationships are linked to decreased recidivism, it can be said that incarceration weakens the protective factors that lower the likelihood of negative outcomes during reentry.

Qualitative research has produced descriptive information about the impact of incarceration on couples and families that is relevant to clinical practice. In particular, it has highlighted male prisoners' dependence on family members, significant others, and cohabiting or marital partners to meet their emotional as well as basic needs during detention (Comfort et al., 2016). These relationships provide human connection in addition to toiletries, money, and extra food. Prisoners' needs put a strain on significant others; as a result, male prisoners may solicit resources from multiple female partners, which can lead to interpersonal conflict. The cost of phone calls and in-person visits also is a major barrier to maintaining contact during incarceration. The lack of communication fuels prisoners' concerns about their partner's loyalty and can increase mistrust in couple relationships. An ethnographic study of low-level justice involvement (i.e., arrests, jail stays, and community supervision) showed that families experienced unique hardships linked to repeated short-term incarceration (Comfort, 2016). Recurrent transitions from jail to the community undermine individuals' progress toward residential and employment stability: When offenders come in and out of jail for short periods of time, they often lose their belongings (e.g., clothes, car) and their identification papers; they can also lose access to government assistance such as the Supplemental Nutrition Assistance Program. Compared with prisoners, they are less likely to participate in educational and mental health programs and to receive medical care during short jail stays. They return to their families with extremely high needs for material and psychological resources, including monitoring and crisis intervention, which drains family resources and produces high levels of stress.

Impact on Parents and Children

A considerable amount of research has examined the effects of parental incarceration on children's and youths' behavioral and mental health outcomes. The findings show a link between parental incarceration and externalizing behaviors in childhood and adolescence. The impact of parental incarceration depends on the amount and quality of parent–child contact before confinement as well as the combination of risk and protective factors in the children's and youths' environment (Geller et al., 2012). Children of incarcerated parents are more likely to experience deep poverty and to be exposed to delinquency, crime, family victimization, and parental substance use (Aaron & Dallaire, 2010). Poverty, community violence, and parents' mental illness and substance use problems have a negative effect on children's well-being distinct from parental incarceration (Turney & Goodsell, 2018).

Researchers estimate that most children of incarcerated parents (60%) will develop low-severity behavioral problems (Kjellstrand et al., 2019; Kjellstrand et al., 2020); however, compared with their peers, they are at higher risk for antisocial behaviors and internalizing problems linked to substance use and delinquency (Kjellstrand et al., 2020; Murray et al., 2012; Wakefield & Powell, 2016). They also are more likely to display increased levels of aggression after paternal incarceration, if they did not witness domestic violence and if their father lived with them before imprisonment (Geller et al., 2012). The evidence suggests that family processes may explain the association between parental incarceration and children's delinquent behaviors (Aaron & Dallaire, 2010): Parental incarceration was found to predict family conflict and family victimization; after controlling for these two variables, the link between parental incarceration and children's delinquency was no longer significant. Research also suggests that boys are more vulnerable to the negative influence of paternal incarceration (Wakefield & Powell, 2016). The size of the effects on aggression was twice as large for boys than for girls (Geller et al., 2012). The scientific literature also describes the effects of parental incarceration on children's increased risk for confinement in a juvenile facility, lower educational attainment, school suspension and expulsion, depression, and poor health in adulthood (Martin, 2017; Turney & Goodsell, 2018). Again, qualitative research has yielded important insight into children's subjective experience of justice contact, parental incarceration, and family visitation behind bars; these are perceived as traumatic events and associated with negative feelings such as anger, resentment, confusion, and fear (Comfort et al., 2016; Murray et al., 2012; C. J. Smith & Young, 2017). Symptoms of posttraumatic stress disorder (e.g., flashbacks) were also reported in response to having witnessed police use weapons and handcuff parents during their arrest (Murray et al., 2012). During parental incarceration, the lack of everyday parent–child interactions and sharing of affection produces a sense of ambiguous loss that can cause grief and other forms of psychological distress (C. J. Smith & Young, 2017). The parent–child relationship becomes less engaged and connected as contact becomes less frequent. Parental absence also leads to changes in family roles and responsibilities that may persist after family reunification (Datchi et al., 2016; C. J. Smith & Young, 2017).

IMPLICATIONS FOR CLINICAL PRACTICE WITH SAM, SARA, GABRIEL, AND JULIA

Table 3.1 offers a summary of the risk and protective factors that are linked to offending in adolescence and adulthood. It will serve to identify the stressors that increase Sam's, Sara's, Gabriel's, and Julia's vulnerability to negative outcomes as well as their resources and strengths. It will also guide the description of their presenting problems and the formulation of hypotheses for further assessment. The next section discusses the risk and protective factors that exist at different levels of the family's ecology: environmental, relational, and individual.

Environmental Factors

Sara and the children reside in a low-income disadvantaged neighborhood where they are exposed to community and school violence (e.g., gang activities). Sam's incarceration has put a strain on the family's economic resources: Sam is unable to bring in an income; phone calls to the jail are $1 per minute; and visitation hours require that Sara take time off work, which results in lost wages. Antisocial peer influence is an area of concern for Gabriel; it appears to support his substance use and delinquent behaviors that led

TABLE 3.1. Factors Linked to Offending and Justice Involvement

Type of factor	Individual	Familial	Environmental
Stable risk factors	Impulsivity as personality trait Problems with hyperactivity and inattention (attention-deficit/ hyperactivity disorder) Low IQ (within the borderline-to-low average range) Sensation seeking Risk taking Low empathy and remorse (callousness) History of victimization	Family criminal history (e.g., parental incarceration) Low family income Large family size Family breakdown (e.g., divorce)	Neighborhood violence (exposure to) Neighborhood socioeconomic disadvantage Neighborhood residential instability Racial discrimination Antisocial peer influence
Dynamic risk factors	Low self-control Weak self-regulation Poor self-esteem Poor self-concept Procriminal attitudes, values, beliefs Poor academic performance Substance use	Family conflict Poor communication Low family cohesion Family violence (intimate partner violence, child abuse and neglect) Harsh parenting Weak parent-child attachment (quality of mother-child bond) Low parental supervision and monitoring Parental attitudes favorable to offending Parental substance use and severe mental illness Parental stress	Association with delinquent peers
Protective factors	Positive attitude toward school Agreeableness Conscientiousness Foresight Low hyperactivity Academic achievement	Familial religiosity High family cohesion Parental warmth Parental support Stable, supportive cohabiting or marital relationship	Neighborhood collective efficacy Prosocial peer relationships (low peer delinquency)

to his involvement with the juvenile justice system. It may also be an issue for Julia, who is using marijuana with her boyfriend. A systemic assessment of the family will determine the severity of Gabriel's and Julia's drug use and whether it results in major impairments that warrant alcohol and drug abuse treatment.

Contact with the justice system and parental incarceration are sources of shame for Julia, and it is possible the family has experienced social stigma that weakened their prosocial involvement in the community. Julia's feelings about her father's incarceration and her efforts to keep it a secret may have pushed her to reduce participation in extracurricular activities (e.g., ballet classes, book club, volunteering in a nursing home) in which other adults monitored her activities and modeled prosocial behaviors. As a result, Julia's exposure to sibling delinquency and antisocial peer influence may have increased. Sara is a member of her neighborhood's Baptist church, which constitutes a resource for the family's material and spiritual needs. The church may also represent a place where the family can develop a positive sense of affiliation and belonging.

Relational Factors

In Sam's absence, Sara has been assuming the family roles of primary provider and caregiver. She works both day and evening shifts at her nursing job, which may limit her capacity to provide consistent parental monitoring and establish stable family routines (e.g., regular family dinners). Sara, Gabriel, and Julia are seldom in the same place at the same time. Sara's day shifts start early, before Gabriel and Julia go to school; likewise, her evening shifts begin at 4:00 p.m., and she has to leave for work before the children get home. Very often, Gabriel plays truant to hang out with his friends in the street, and every day after school Julia spends time with her boyfriend. The family is struggling to maintain a sense of connectedness while managing the material and emotional costs of Sam's incarceration. Sara carries the weight of added responsibilities that may exceed her resources, produce distress, exacerbate feelings of loss and anger, and thus diminish her ability to bond with Gabriel and Julia. Parent–child conflict and poor communication also are a concern: They limit Sara's ability to guide and support her children. Couple discord and low levels of trust may further undermine the effectiveness of parenting. Criticism and defensiveness comprise an interaction pattern that often results in heated arguments between Sam and Sara; they also make it difficult to resolve disagreements about parenting and everyday life. Despite their differences, both Sam and Sara share a sense of responsibility for the family's well-being; they also see family loyalty as a value and a priority.

Individual Factors

At the individual level, Sam's risk factors include a history of criminal activities, exposure to childhood traumatic events, substance misuse, and severe posttraumatic stress disorder. In the context of the family, Sara's substance use and parenting stress are individual factors that increase the odds that her children will engage in delinquency. Gabriel appears to display procriminal attitudes when he brags about his father's justice involvement and street smarts. His drinking, emotional disturbance, poor academic performance, and lack of participation in prosocial activities are significant problems to consider in treatment. Julia's academic performance and extracurricular activities and Sara's religiosity may constitute protective factors. The assessment of the family in Chapter 4 further explores the relational dynamics that influence their capacity to manage adverse events successfully to prevent negative outcomes and improve individual and relational functioning.

4 CLINICAL PRACTICE WITH JUSTICE-INVOLVED FAMILIES

Systemic Assessment and Case Conceptualization

The systemic assessment of couples and families involves the use of procedures and instruments to collect data about individuals and their relationships; to develop an understanding of the interpersonal dynamics that influence individual, couple, and family functioning; and to formulate hypotheses about the multilevel factors and processes that contribute to the clinical problem and reason for referral (Stanton & Welsh, 2011). The selection of specific assessment methods and tools often depends on the clinician's treatment model and whether it emphasizes emotions, attachment, meanings, thoughts, beliefs, behaviors, or some combination of these (Lebow, 2014).

Assessment begins with the first contact with the client and continues throughout treatment. It also involves multiple sources of information, such as court intake reports and school and mental health records. In the first session, the two main objectives are to (a) specify the nature and severity of the issues and (b) clarify the focus of therapy (Sperry, 2011). The findings serve as the rationale for clinical recommendations. For the entire duration of treatment, clinicians also evaluate the effects of their interventions on client outcomes to identify new goals and activities (e.g., practicing communication skills), if appropriate.

https://doi.org/10.1037/0000285-005
Best Clinical Practices for Treating Families in Juvenile and Criminal Justice Systems, by C. C. Datchi

This chapter discusses the concepts and methods of systemic assessment and illustrates their application with Sara, Gabriel, and Julia, who were referred to family therapy after Gabriel was arrested for underage drinking and public disturbance. It describes the steps leading to the formulation of the problem (Stanton & Welsh, 2011). It also includes information about commonly used mapping tools and standardized measures that are based on three major theoretical models for the evaluation of couple and family relationships: the McMaster model of family functioning, the circumplex model, and the Beavers systems model. The discussion ends with the case conceptualization of the fictitious family (i.e., Sam, Julia, Gabriel, and Julia). The case conceptualization organizes the information collected during the assessment, offers a systemic understanding of Gabriel's behaviors in the context of the family and the neighborhood, and identifies areas of clinical intervention.

FIRST CONTACT WITH THE FAMILY

Dr. Merlin is a licensed psychologist who provides assessment and treatment services through the Psychological Services Division of the Lake County Judicial Circuit Court. The court intake officer evaluated Gabriel, recommended informal probation and family therapy, and referred Gabriel and his family to the court's Psychological Services Division. When she received the referral, Dr. Merlin reviewed the court intake report and called Sara to schedule the first session. This first contact provided the opportunity to gather preliminary information about the family and to form initial impressions about the presenting problem in the context of the family relationships. Dr. Merlin asked Sara a few questions to determine who would join the meeting and listened for Sara's understanding of the presenting problem. Who lives at home? How does Sara perceive Gabriel's difficulties? Who in the family has expressed concerns about Gabriel? Dr. Merlin noted that Sara was forthcoming about the family's challenges (e.g., parental incarceration, economic instability) and her struggles with parenting teenagers on her own. She also observed that Sara was relieved that the court provided assistance in monitoring Gabriel. Dr. Merlin asked Sara's permission to talk with Gabriel and Julia. Gabriel said very little during the phone conversation except to indicate that he did not think he needed therapy. In an effort to engage Gabriel in treatment, Dr. Merlin acknowledged his view of the situation and suggested they meet at least once with his mother and sister, to discuss what he could do to show the court and his family that he could take care of himself. Gabriel agreed to give it a try. Julia was more responsive than her brother. During the phone conversation, she described her worries about her mother.

The court intake report contained relevant information about Gabriel and his immediate environment. English was the family's primary language at home. Gabriel described his mother as "caring too much." He reported he had a close relationship with his father: Before Sam's incarceration, they would hang out and play basketball. Gabriel was proud of his father because he was "manly and brave." He indicated his relationship with his sister was fair. She and he were different: She liked school and had good grades, whereas he struggled to complete the schoolwork and was placed into special education classes when he was 14. Gabriel's academic difficulties produced frustration and embarrassment that often led to defiant behaviors and conflict with teachers and other adults. Gabriel did not believe he had a substance abuse problem. He reported he drank alcohol ("some beer and liquor") and vaped marijuana (about one quarter of a vape cartridge) approximately twice a week. He denied selling drugs on the street. The intake report included the results of a substance abuse screening measure, which showed Gabriel had a low probability of having a substance use disorder.

The family rented a three-bedroom apartment in a neighborhood where fights and robberies were a concern. At home, Gabriel was expected to help with household tasks (i.e., taking out the trash, making his bed) and to observe an 8:00 p.m. curfew during the week. His mother needed to prompt him to complete his chores, and for the most part he was compliant. However, he regularly stayed out past 9:00 p.m. and sometimes did not come home on the weekends. Gabriel reported his mother would ground him for a week or take his phone away when he broke curfew. He also disclosed he had four close friends with whom he liked to play video games: Two of them used alcohol; the other two had been arrested on charges of robbery. Gabriel acknowledged he drank beer with his friends, three to four cans once a week, and never by himself. Gabriel was not involved in community or school-related activities, and his first sexual experience had occurred at age 14. His score on the Youth Assessment System Disposition tool (Latessa & Lovins, 2012), a measure of criminogenic risk, indicated his overall level of risk for recidivism was low to moderate.

During the court intake, Gabriel appeared in good health, and his attitude was cooperative. He wore clean clothes, maintained appropriate eye contact, and spoke at a normal rate and volume. His speech was coherent, and there were no signs of obsession, compulsions, or deficits in attention and memory. However, Gabriel's insight was limited: He did not think there was anything wrong with his behaviors. He stated his mood was "good," and his affect was slightly restricted but congruent with his mood. He reported he had not received psychological services in the past.

CREATING THE THERAPEUTIC FRAME

During the phone conversation with Sara, Gabriel, and Julia, Dr. Merlin started to create the therapeutic frame: She obtained informed consent for treatment, shared information about the Psychological Services Division of Lake County Court, clarified expectations and policies, and gathered preliminary data. Dr. Merlin informed Sara that services were free; however, the family was responsible for transportation to Dr. Merlin's office, and treatment would be terminated after the family had missed two consecutive sessions. In addition, Dr. Merlin notified Sara and Gabriel that she would report treatment attendance to Gabriel's probation officer.

The first contact also offered the opportunity to develop a therapeutic relationship with the family members and to take note of their perspectives or definitions of the problem. Dr. Merlin acknowledged Sara's experience with an attitude of respect and communicated her appreciation of the family's current conditions: Sara felt betrayed and abandoned when Sam was arrested and sent to jail; she was crumbling under the burden of parenting and financial stress and was at her wit's end with Gabriel; she was also worried she could not protect him from the streets. Dr. Merlin noticed Julia's concerns about her mother, whom she described as moody and irritable. Dr. Merlin wondered about Julia's role in the family system: Had she assumed a caretaking role in the parent–child relationship? Gabriel's silence during the phone conversation was a sign of low motivation. He did not perceive the need for therapy; by limiting communication, he formed a boundary that protected him from adult interference. The initial contact yielded insight into the effects of Sam's justice involvement on the family's interpersonal dynamics and individual well-being. It also provided valuable data about family engagement, one of the four dimensions of the therapeutic alliance in couple and family therapy (the others being an emotional connection with the therapist, a feeling of safety in the therapeutic system, and a shared sense of purpose; these are discussed in the following sections).

THE THERAPEUTIC ALLIANCE

The therapeutic alliance is a critical ingredient of effective interventions; it has been linked to positive results in clinical practice with couples and families (Friedlander et al., 2018). It consists of four dimensions: (a) family engagement, (b) emotional connection with the clinician, (c) a feeling of safety in the therapeutic system, and (d) a shared sense of purpose (Friedlander et al., 2006). The therapeutic alliance is a mechanism of change that operates at multiple levels of the therapeutic system (Lebow, 2014): between the therapist and the couple or family as a unit (the *shared alliance*), between the therapist and each individual in the couple or family (the *therapist–client alliance*), and between partners or family members (the *within-family alliance*). There is a reciprocal relation between the different levels of the therapeutic alliance such that each level influences the development and maintenance of other levels during treatment. They are also influenced by each family member's perceptions of the clinician's relationship with other family members (the *other alliance*).

The evidence suggests that different levels of the alliance predict retention and outcomes in empirically supported family therapy programs for adolescents with substance use and externalizing behavior problems (Datchi & Sexton, 2016); specifically, research shows that in functional family therapy it is the shared alliance that contributes to reduced youth substance use in Hispanic families, not Anglo families (Flicker et al., 2008). In multidimensional family therapy, the effects of the therapist–youth alliance on youth's behaviors have been shown to depend on the strength of the therapist–parent alliance early in treatment (Hogue & Liddle, 2009). (Chapter 5 provides an in-depth discussion of functional family therapy and multidimensional family therapy.) These findings highlight the contingent nature of relational processes and their effects on client outcomes: The level and strength of the therapeutic alliance that matter most depend on the type of therapeutic programs as well as cultural factors.

Family Engagement

Engagement is a concept that describes clients' attitudes and behaviors in therapy (Becker et al., 2014; Friedlander et al., 2006); specifically, it refers to their view of therapeutic services as valuable and useful as well as their level of participation in sessions (e.g., working with the provider toward agreed-on goals). Engagement is a dynamic process that fluctuates over time and is linked to the other three dimensions of the therapeutic alliance; clients' treatment satisfaction; environmental barriers, such as cost of transportation, housing instability, family responsibilities, family socioeconomic disadvantage; and diversity factors, such as race, ethnicity, gender, and age (Becker et al., 2014; Ofonedu et al., 2017; O'Keeffe et al., 2019; Roos & Werbart, 2013). Becker and colleagues (2014) found that race was a predictor of initial engagement in a sample of youths and caregivers who participated in behavioral health programming: Specifically, engagement levels were lower for Black youths compared with Whites. A meta-analysis of adult psychotherapy studies also showed a significant association among age, educational attainment, and premature termination (Swift & Greenberg, 2012): On average, clients who discontinued treatment were younger and had less education. The quality of the therapeutic alliance is a well-established predictor of engagement (Roos & Werbart, 2013): Clients are more likely to stay in treatment when the alliance is strong, and they are more likely to drop out when they disagree with the clinician on the definition of the problem and the goals and tasks of therapy.

In clinical practice with couples and families, engagement is both an essential and complex process (Friedlander et al., 2006): It involves multiple individuals with diverse perspectives and different goals, who may enter treatment voluntarily or not and with different levels of motivation. For example, Sara sees Sam's criminal history as a major cause of Gabriel's delinquent behaviors, Julia views Sara's mood as the problem, and Gabriel perceives treatment as a form of intrusion and a threat to his lifestyle. Sara's goal is to change Gabriel, whereas Gabriel wishes he could get out of therapy. Likewise, Julia does not see the utility of treatment and would rather spend more time with her boyfriend. Gabriel and his mother were mandated to seek mental health and family services, and none of the family members initiated treatment willingly. To engage them in the therapeutic process, Dr. Merlin had to create conditions that instilled hope and supported family collaboration as soon as the first session.

Family collaboration is a key aspect of evidence-based family therapies for youth with conduct disorders (see Chapter 5 for a review of these treatment models; Tuerk et al., 2012). Specific strategies to foster family engagement as well as collaboration include

- *reflective listening*, or acknowledging the family members' individual experience in a way that communicates understanding, respect, caring and warmth;
- *reframing*, or attributing new meanings to interpersonal events and behaviors to increase tolerance or acceptance;
- *positive reinforcement* that highlights small behavioral changes in session and promotes self-efficacy and optimism;
- *identifying and building on couple and family strengths*; and

- *maintaining a relational (vs. individual) focus* (e.g., understanding how the problem works in the couple or family, accommodating the family's need for flexible scheduling so that they can attend treatment together; Lebow, 2014; Sexton, 2016; Tuerk et al., 2012).

These strategies can be used to both engage and motivate justice-involved youth, adults, and families, who generally have lower rates of treatment participation and completion.

Client engagement is a major concern in clinical practice with correctional populations. Research suggests that dropout rates range from approximately 27% to 38% for the treatment of offenders and are as high as 45% for the treatment of adolescents (O'Keeffe et al., 2019; Olver et al., 2011). Several factors account for the difficulty to initiate and retain in treatment: Services are mandated rather than voluntary, offenders may perceive treatment as a sanction rather than a resource, and they may minimize the problem and have low levels of motivation for change (S. J. Thompson et al., 2007).

To engage Sara, Gabriel, and Julia, Dr. Merlin invited the family into a conversation that highlighted the underlying feelings and motives for their behaviors and created a shared definition of the problem: Gabriel is seeking belonging as well as independence; Sara is holding on to her family by a thread and is scared of losing her children to the streets; the family is fighting the effects of loss, grief, and trauma. In the first session, Dr. Merlin showed curiosity about and interest in their respective perspectives and experiences of the problem, focused on their interpretations of what happened between them, and created new meanings for their difficulties. She also praised them for their willingness to explore new avenues for solutions and worked with the family to define the problem and specify the goals and activities of treatment.

Emotional Connection With the Clinician

The concept of *emotional connection* describes the personal bond that develops between the therapist and the client over the course of treatment. It also reflects the qualities of the therapeutic relationship: Family members form an emotional connection with the clinician when they experience warmth, neutrality, a nonjudgmental approach, acceptance, a calm presence, and a relaxed attitude (S. J. Thompson et al., 2007). Friedlander and colleagues (2006) compared the therapeutic bond to a type of kinship based on trust and caring as well as appreciation for the provider's expertise. To foster emotional connection, clinicians use a variety of strategies, including humor, empathic responding, a mimicking of the family's mannerisms, and acting in ways that are congruent with the family structure and transactional patterns. They use these techniques to join with the family members and intervene from within as a member of the therapeutic system they create with the family.

When treatment has been ordered by the legal system or other institutions, families may view therapy as a form of punishment, which poses a challenge to emotional connection. Sara, Gabriel, and Julia had not received psychological services before meeting with Dr. Merlin, and they were not familiar with the therapeutic process. Given their involvement with the criminal justice system, they were also wary of government officials in general. Gabriel expressed an unwillingness to attend the first session, Julia felt like a hostage who was paying the price for Gabriel's mistakes, and Sara saw mandated treatment as yet another complication in her everyday life. In the first session, Dr. Merlin described her role in relation to the court and reminded the family of her obligation to report on attendance. She demonstrated respect for and understanding of the family members' viewpoints: The family was required to participate in psychological services, and it felt like an intrusion into their personal life; it is not surprising they were upset and concerned about their privacy. Sara had mixed feelings about treatment for Gabriel: On the one hand, it may change Gabriel's behaviors and thus keep him out of the justice system; on the other, she worried it would create additional burden. Dr. Merlin maintained the focus on the family as she joined with them by acknowledging and normalizing their thoughts and feelings. To foster collaboration, she also adopted a low-power position in the therapeutic relationship and made space for each family member to voice their concerns and discuss goals.

Sense of Safety in the Therapeutic System

Feeling safe is a necessary condition for individuals to take risks and try new behaviors, such as talking about painful emotions (Friedlander et al., 2006). It is related to trust in both the couple and family relationships and the therapeutic system. It is also determined by the communication patterns and level of negativity in the couple and family. When partners or family members disagree on the definition of the problem, and blame each other with criticism and defensiveness, their conversations often result in increased strain that weakens their relational bonds and create an atmosphere of hostility. Chapter 3 described the effects of justice involvement on couple and family relationships and emotions in particular. Anger and resentment, along with embarrassment, shame, and mistrust, are common responses to criminal behaviors and incarceration. How the clinician manages negativity and conflict with justice-involved couples and families is critical to feelings of safety.

In the first session, Dr. Merlin observed Sara, Gabriel, and Julia's interactions and noted that Gabriel became visibly angry and defensive when Sara complained about his behaviors and his father's. The tension increased rapidly between them; both mother and son appeared overwhelmed with negative feelings, and their exchanges exacerbated emotional flooding (experiencing overwhelming feelings and physiological arousal) and conflict. Dr. Merlin also noticed how Julia withdrew during the argument: She pulled out her smartphone and began texting. Blaming and hostility created an unsafe environment that restricted family engagement and emotional connection. Dr. Merlin used the technique of *reframing* to interrupt negative mother–son transactions; specifically, she talked about Gabriel's anger: She saw how he stood up to defend Sam; clearly, he would not allow anyone, including his family, to paint a bad picture of his father. He was loyal to Sam no matter what. Dr. Merlin also addressed Sara's complaints and her fear of losing her child to the criminal justice system. Sara felt the loss of Sam's incarceration and could not bear the thought of being separated from Gabriel. These statements highlight the positive intentions behind Gabriel's and Sara's behaviors; they reframe the parent–child interactions to increase tolerance and reduce emotional reactivity in family relationships. It is easier to remain unaffected by anger and criticism when it is clear that family members are acting to protect each other.

Shared Sense of Purpose

Couples and families share a sense of purpose when they agree on the nature of their problems and the goals of treatment, when they perceive therapy as a valuable strategy to address their difficulties, and when they engage in therapeutic tasks as a cohesive unit (Friedlander et al., 2006, 2018; Lambert et al., 2012). The concept of shared sense of purpose refers to the within-family processes of the therapeutic alliance, or *within-family alliance* (Friedlander et al., 2006). It is linked to perceived progress early in therapy, feelings of safety, and treatment retention (Friedlander et al., 2014). Together with engagement, it is also a primary focus of clinical interventions with clients who have been mandated into treatment (Sotero et al., 2017). Families who are required to enter treatment often have different levels of motivation and different perspectives on the problem; these differences limit their ability to work together toward a common goal.

In the initial session, Sara, Gabriel, and Julia discussed the reason why they had been referred to psychological services. Their conversation showed they did not see eye to eye: Gabriel did not think the family needed therapy, Julia attended treatment to support her mother, and Sara wished her son would do as he was told. To foster a shared sense of purpose, Dr. Merlin highlighted the family's similar feelings, needs, and perceptions of what might resolve their concerns: They were angry their family was caught in the net of the justice system; they were also worrying about losing more loved ones to detention or incarceration; and they needed safety and autonomy from external influence; however, they struggled to protect the family from outside intervention. Dr. Merlin acknowledged each individual viewpoint while emphasizing the need for family-based solutions to the problem, that is, what Sara, Julia, and Gabriel could do together to disentangle the family from the justice system and avoid further disruption.

CONDUCTING A SYSTEMIC ASSESSMENT

To understand clients' distress in the context of couple and family relationships, clinicians use various methods of assessment and gather qualitative and quantitative data about the couple and family system from the perspective of each individual in treatment. In the first session, they conduct a clinical interview and facilitate a conversation with and between the family members to observe their interactions. They evaluate relational functioning in six central areas (Bray, 2009; Stanton & Welsh, 2011). The first area is the *family structure*; it refers to family membership (i.e., who belongs to the family) and type (e.g., cohabiting couple, divorced family). The second area is *family organization*; it includes the rules or boundaries that define how individuals carry out their roles or functions (e.g., parent, sibling) in the family system. The third is *family affect* or *emotional expression*. The fourth corresponds to the *relational patterns* or *stable behavioral exchanges* in which the family members engage repeatedly over time. The *outcomes* of these transactions (e.g., connectedness, distance, authority or power) constitute the fifth area. The last domain covers *diversity factors* in treatment. (For a discussion of diversity factors in the justice system, see Chapter 2.) During the initial session, clinicians also assess the family's cognitions, specifically, the meanings they attribute to others' actions that influence their emotional and behavioral response (Lebow, 2014; Williams et al., 2011).

As mentioned in Chapter 2, *diversity* defines the broader social and cultural context of face-to-face interactions in everyday life. It includes gender, sexuality, ethnicity, race, class, religion, generational and immigration status, and culture. Cultural norms, beliefs, and values influence individuals' perception of self and others, the nature of their familial and social relationships, the meanings they attribute to events, and their emotional responses to situations. They also determine attitudes toward help-seeking and formal institutions and how the person understands and addresses problematic behaviors (McGoldrick & Ashton, 2012).

Cultural and social diversity define the context in which clinicians develop a therapeutic relationship with couples and families and conduct a systemic assessment. Culturally competent practice requires that therapists be aware of their own assumptions about family processes, that they be curious about their clients' worldview and value system, and that they be willing to discuss diversity factors in treatment (Stanton & Welsh, 2011). The next section describes how Dr. Merlin conducted a systemic assessment of the relationships among Sara, Sam, Gabriel, and Julia, and how she incorporated considerations of diversity into the development of the therapeutic relationship. It is followed by a discussion of commonly used qualitative and standardized measures in systemic assessment.

The Clinical Interview

In the first session, Dr. Merlin observed the interactions and communication among Sara, Gabriel, and Julia, and began to formulate hypotheses about the boundaries and hierarchy or power structure of the family system. The following questions guided the assessment; they are consistent with empirical knowledge about the predictors of antisocial conduct (see Table 3.1 in Chapter 3):

- How direct and clear is family communication?
- How do family members start and resolve conflict?
- What are the levels of closeness, warmth, and affection in family exchanges?
- How much support does the family offer each other?
- Who has more power in the family?
- Does the family hierarchy promote optimal functioning? In particular, does it allow Sara to properly monitor her children and influence their behaviors?

Dr. Merlin also paid attention to Julia's role in Sara's and Gabriel's relationship in the presence of parent–child conflict. What was Julia's responsibility for the well-being of the family and the emotional needs of her mother in particular?

During the clinical interview, Dr. Merlin asked questions to determine how family members experienced and understood the presenting problem:

- How does the family explain their referral to treatment?
- Whom have they told about the referral?
- Who is most worried about the problem that brought the family to treatment?
- When did the problem begin?
- When does it occur?
- Who does what when the problem happens?
- How has the family tried to resolve their concerns?
- Have there been any recent changes in the family?

In clinical practice with justice-involved families, the clinical interview may take the form of a conversation with the family rather than a question-and-answer session. The therapist's conversational style, whereby they acknowledge the importance of the family members' feelings and beliefs about the problem in a personal way, and when family members perceive that the therapist is working hard to understand them, facilitates family engagement (Sexton, 2016; Sheehan & Friedlander, 2015).

There are salient differences between Dr. Merlin and the family. Dr. Merlin is a White, middle-age, female psychologist born in the United States who comes from a middle-class background. Sara, Gabriel, and Julia are an intercultural family of mixed national, racial, and ethnic origins. They describe their economic status as low middle-class. The success of the family's treatment depends on Dr. Merlin's ability to form a therapeutic alliance with *cultural humility*: the clinician's self-reflexivity, willingness to examine assumptions and values, capacity to regulate emotional reactions to cultural differences, to show interest in and respect for families' worldview, and to address power imbalances in the therapeutic relationship (Holyoak et al., 2020). In the first session, Dr. Merlin communicated cultural humility by asking questions about family-of-origin and cultural values. After meeting with Sara, Gabriel, and Julia, she reflected on her experience and examined how biases might shape her view of the family and the problem. In addition, she considered whether cultural differences in the family were a source of stress, for example, whether they had an effect on the communication among Sara, Sam, and the children. Intercultural couples face unique challenges and experience greater levels of conflict and instability than monocultural couples. They may experience disapproval from their families of origin and communities, including racism (Linhof & Allan, 2019). They may feel torn between their loyalty to their family of origin and their commitment to their partner. They may also disagree about family rituals, holiday celebrations, affective expression in public and private places, and the distribution of family responsibilities (Holzapfel et al., 2018). In the first session, Dr. Merlin explored these areas of family life; in particular, she asked Sara, Gabriel, and Julia to describe how they celebrated important events in the family and how they made decisions about household tasks. She also inquired about the role of Sam's and Sara's families of origin in their everyday life.

Commonly Used Measures in Systemic Assessment

In conducting a systemic assessment, clinicians use mapping tools such as the genogram and the social network map (see Figure 4.1) to explore the broader context of the family and identify social resources, core beliefs, intergenerational themes, and developmental issues that are relevant to the presenting problems. (For more details about qualitative assessment in couple and family therapy, see McGoldrick et al., 2020; Sperry, 2011; Thomlison, 2016; and Williams et al., 2011.) They also administer self-report standardized instruments to collect baseline data about specific areas of functioning and to track change over the course of treatment.

The most commonly used standardized measures of family functioning are based on three transtheoretical models (E. Hamilton & Carr, 2016): the

FIGURE 4.1. The Family's Social Network Map

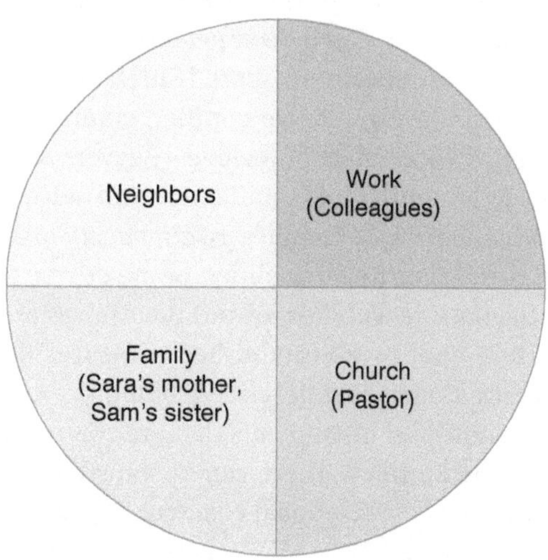

McMaster model of family functioning (Epstein et al., 2003; Ryan et al., 2005), the circumplex model of marital and family systems (Olson & Gorall, 2003), and the Beavers systems model (Beavers & Hampson, 2003). According to the McMaster model, clinical problems develop when the family is not able to manage basic, developmental, and hazardous tasks effectively (e.g., providing food, becoming parents, dealing with illness). Problem solving, communication, behavior control (i.e., the rules that govern behaviors), role allocation and accountability (i.e., how family members hold each other accountable for meeting their responsibilities), and affective responsiveness and involvement (i.e., show of interest in each other) are the core areas of family functioning (Ryan et al., 2005). They vary on a continuum from most effective, where they support optimal health, to most ineffective, where they contribute to clinical problems. The circumplex model focuses on three dimensions of marital and family systems: (a) cohesion, (b) flexibility, and (c) communication (Olson & Gorall, 2003). *Cohesion* is the process of emotional bonding and the balance between closeness and distance in couple and family relationships. *Flexibility* represents the couple or family's ability to balance change and stability in leadership, roles, and relationship rules. *Communication* encompasses families' listening skills, self-disclosure or sharing of feelings, speaking clearly and for oneself rather than for others, staying on topic, and showing respect and regard.

In balanced types of couple and family systems, leadership is democratic and involves negotiation and shared decision making; change in roles and rules is developmentally appropriate and allows the effective management of new conditions (e.g., adolescents' need for increased autonomy). Balanced couples and families are expected to manage developmental transitions and situational stress more effectively. The Beavers systems model emphasizes two relational constructs: (a) family competence and (b) relational styles. *Family competence* is the capacity to share leadership, create appropriate intergenerational boundaries, resolve conflict, communicate openly and directly, and express a wide range of feelings (Beavers & Hampson, 2003). It is presumed to foster individual confidence and self-esteem as well as system adaptation and growth. Families' *relational styles* are characterized by their centripetal and centrifugal qualities, or the degree to which they are oriented toward the outside world or toward themselves as a unit. Table 4.1 presents information about well-established measures that are based on the three assessment models just described. Table 4.1 and Table 4.2 both include a list of standardized instruments that are commonly used to assess couple and family relationships. These can be valuable tools to determine the nature and severity of the relational concerns of justice-involved clients.

TABLE 4.1. Commonly Used Self-Report Instruments for Family Assessment

Instrument name	Construct measured	Population considerations
Self-Report Family Assessment Device (Ryan et al., 2005)	Based on the McMaster model of family functioning; measures problem solving, communication, roles, affective responsiveness, affective involvement, behavior control	Normed on families of medical and psychiatric patients; for family members 12 years and older
Circumplex Model Family Adaptability and Cohesion Evaluation Scale IV (Olson, 2011)	Based on the circumplex model of family functioning; measures family cohesion, flexibility, communication	Information about scale validity based on a convenience sample of undergraduate university students; for family members 12 years and older
Beavers Self-Report Family Inventory (Beavers & Hampson, 2000)	Based on the Beavers systems model; measures family competence (structure and flexibility) and family interaction style	Information about reliability and validity based on diverse clinical and nonclinical samples (families of patients with schizophrenia and borderline personality disorder; ethnically diverse nonclinical families; parents of lesbian, gay, and bisexual children; university students); for family members 11 years and older
Family Assessment Measure-III (Skinner et al., 2000)	Based on the process model of family functioning; measures task accomplishment, role performance, affective involvement, control, norms and values, and communication/affective expression	Information about reliability and validity obtained from clinical and nonclinical community samples (university students, families, mothers, fathers, children, adults and adolescents); for family members 10 years and older
Family Environment Scale (Moos, 2009)	Based on the social systems ecological model of family functioning; measures three dimensions of the family environment: (a) family relationship (commitment, support, emotional expression, and conflict and negativity), (b) personal growth (individual autonomy, values and interests), and (c) systems maintenance (family organization and control)	Information about psychometric properties obtained from clinical and nonclinical samples (families of chronically ill children, mothers, fathers, adolescents, undergraduate students); for family members 11 years and older

(continues)

TABLE 4.1. Commonly Used Self-Report Instruments for Family Assessment (*Continued*)

Instrument name	Construct measured	Population considerations
Systemic Clinical Outcome and Routine Evaluation (Carr & Stratton, 2017)	Based on general family systems theory; measures treatment outcomes in four areas: (a) family strengths, (b) difficulties, (c) communication, and (d) adjustment	Development and validation based on information obtained from community samples in the United Kingdom, Ireland, Poland, and Portugal (university students; families; adults in inpatient and outpatient mental health services; lesbian, gay, and bisexual individuals; detained male and female juvenile offenders); for family members 7 years and older

Clinicians should also remember that these couple and family assessment measures were not developed for and standardized on correctional populations, with the exception of the Systemic Clinical Outcome and Routine Evaluation (Carr & Stratton, 2017; see Table 4.1). As a result, they may not be sensitive to salient aspects of justice involvement that have an impact on couple and family functioning (see Chapter 3).

The selection of assessment tools depends on the concepts that are pertinent to specific clinical problems and populations. In clinical practice with justice-involved couples and families, therapists focus on the risk and protective factors that predict delinquency and criminal conduct (see Chapter 3). In particular, they choose measures to identify the perpetuating processes that maintain justice involvement in the family's everyday life. In the case of Sara, Sam, Gabriel, and Julia, Chapter 3 highlighted several risk factors: parent–child conflict, couple discord, poor family communication, substance use, mental illness, exposure to traumatic events, antisocial peer influence, and financial strain. To evaluate the family's rules, roles, communication, and problem solving, Dr. Merlin selected the Family Assessment Device (FAD), a self-report standardized instrument that measures individuals' perception of their family's functioning on the six dimensions of the McMaster model (Epstein et al., 1983). The FAD is completed by family members age 12 and older. A considerable amount of research shows that it is a reliable and valid assessment tool that identifies strength and problem areas (E. Hamilton & Carr, 2016). The General Functioning scale of the FAD can be used to track change over the course of therapy (Mansfield et al.,

TABLE 4.2. Commonly Used Self-Report Instruments for Measuring Dyadic Adjustment

Instrument name	Construct measured	Population considerations
Dyadic Assessment Scale (Spanier, 1976)	Measures relationship adjustment in four domains: (a) dyadic consensus, (b) dyadic satisfaction, (c) affectional expression, and (d) dyadic cohesion	Normed on samples of married, divorced, and never-married cohabiting couples; 18 years and older
Locke Wallace Marital Adjustment Test (Locke & Wallace, 1959)	Measures general marital satisfaction and level of agreement on common issues that produce conflict in couple relationships	Information about psychometric properties based on community samples of White married couples and caregivers of patients with cancer; 18 years and older
Enriching Relationship Issues, Communication and Happiness (Fowers & Olson, 1993)	Measures couple satisfaction, communication, and conflict resolution	Information about reliability and validity based on ethnically and culturally diverse married adults; 18 years and older
Marital Satisfaction Inventory-Revised (D. K. Snyder, 1997)	Measures relationship distress and strengths in several domains: overall distress, affective communication, problem solving, aggression, time spent on shared activities, disagreement about finances, sexual dissatisfaction, role orientation, family history of distress, dissatisfaction with children, conflict over child rearing	Standardized on sample of intact, heterosexual couples; 18 years and older

Note. Dyadic adjustment is a concept that defines relationship quality as partners' ability to accommodate their differences, reach a consensus, and foster positivity in their interactions.

2019). Dr. Merlin also chose the Strengths and Difficulties Questionnaire (SDQ; Goodman, 1997, 2001), a brief instrument with good reliability and validity across diverse samples, that evaluates adolescent functioning, ages 11 to 17, on five dimensions: (a) Emotional Symptoms, (b) Conduct Problems, (c) Hyperactivity/Inattention, (d) Peer Relationship Difficulties, and (e) Prosocial Behaviors. There are several versions of the SDQ: Julia and Gabriel completed the self-report version, one form for each child, and Sara completed the parent version. The objectives were to assess Julia's and Gabriel's level of difficulties from multiple perspectives and evaluate treatment outcomes. Dr. Merlin instructed the family to complete the measures online before the second session.

CASE CONCEPTUALIZATION

This section organizes the quantitative and qualitative data Dr. Merlin collected about Sara and Sam's family and discusses the concerns from a systemic perspective. The information is arranged into six categories: (a) the presenting problem, (b) pertinent family and individual history, (c) predisposing factors, (d) precipitating factors or identifiable stressors, (e) perpetuating factors, and (f) past treatment (Stanton & Welsh, 2011). The case formulation includes data derived from Gabriel's intake report, the clinical interview, the standardized assessment measures (i.e., Youth Assessment System Disposition [YAS; Latessa & Lovins, 2012], FAD, SDQ), and the social network map. The objectives are to explain the family's difficulties, identify their strengths, and highlight areas of interventions.

The Presenting Problem

Sara, Gabriel, and Julia had different perspectives on the problem that brought them into treatment; however, they could all agree on one thing: The family's contact with the juvenile and criminal justice system compromised their integrity and autonomy; it was a major stressor that produced tension, conflict, and negativity, including shame, anger, and fear. The family members made many attempts to protect themselves and each other as well as their relationships. Julia walked away from arguments between her mother and Gabriel. She also made herself small, to ease Sara's burden, and kept a worried eye on her mother; she vacuumed, washed the dishes, did the laundry, and prepared meals during the work week. After Sam's incarceration, she took on more responsibility at home to preserve some sense of stability and order amidst the family disruption. When Sam was sent to jail, Gabriel became the man of the family, a leadership role he took pride in. However, at 15 he was not prepared to become the protector of the household. He still needed guidance and support in learning to problem-solve and make decisions. The authority he gained from becoming the man of the family interfered with parental influence: Gabriel believed he had to show strength and independence and identify solutions on his own; drinking and acting tough bolstered his masculine identity. Sara worried about paying the bills, putting food on the table, and keeping her children safe while responding to Sam's requests for emotional and material assistance. She maintained frequent contact with Sam, took his calls, visited him, and deposited money into his commissary account. She was holding on to her family and stretched to the limit as she tried to fulfill her family roles. Her distress and mixed feelings about Sam's incarceration and related family changes complicated her efforts to support Gabriel and Julia's positive youth development. According to Sara, she and Sam had similar views on parenting: Both emphasized family ties, respect, politeness, deference and obedience to elders, or what Sam called *familismo* and *respeto* (see Ayón et al., 2015, and Calzada et al., 2010). However, Sara perceived Sam to be more traditional in his roles as partner and father: He expected Gabriel and Julia to stay quiet when he set limits or reprimanded them, whereas Sara allowed the children to politely express disagreement. Sara was more responsive to Julia's and Gabriel's needs for greater autonomy. In some measure, the family struggled to navigate cultural differences, which resulted in marital and parent–child conflict.

The family's scores on the FAD highlighted skill deficits in communication and problem solving as well as low levels of affective involvement and ineffective behavior control. Family communication was direct but masked; figuratively speaking, family members did not hear the content of their verbal exchanges. They were not able to discuss their concerns and identify the problem. In addition, they showed little interest in their respective activities. They had clear rules for good behaviors; however, they did not have strategies to encourage adherence. Gabriel's scores on the YAS suggested that Sara did not consistently set age-appropriate boundaries or follow through with consequences. It also showed that Gabriel was often unwilling to follow her rules.

Pertinent Family and Individual History

In Chapter 2, the family's history highlighted two clinical issues that warrant attention in treatment: (a) trauma and (b) substance use. Traumatic experiences have a negative effect on a person's ability to regulate anxiety and anger; they also influence their perceptions of the environment as unsafe or unpredictable and can result in relationship mistrust and isolation as well as destructive coping strategies (e.g., drinking, using drugs; Johnson, 2002). A person's response to adversity often depends on the quality of their bonds with significant others. Secure emotional connections have been found to promote healing from trauma (Dalton et al., 2013; Weissman et al., 2018). In the case of Sara and Sam's family, parent–child conflict, family disruption, and instability are conditions that diminish the family members' capacity to deal with adverse experiences. Gabriel's substance use started after age 12 and was linked to his association with antisocial peers. It was a clinical concern to the extent that it led to his arrest and informal probation. It had a negative impact on Gabriel's social outcomes but did not meet the criteria for a psychiatric disorder. Parental substance use is a predisposing or risk factor that will be discussed in the family's next session with Dr. Merlin.

The family history suggests that intergroup bias and social stigma in the family of origin had an impact on the couple's dynamics. Sara explained that her parents and siblings were opposed to her marrying outside of her cultural group. She described family hostility and rejection that resulted in social isolation and increased stress and limited the couple's ability to form a safe connection. She also reported frequent arguments about Sam's "overinvolvement" with his family of origin, which prevented the couple from forming a unified partnership with a strong sense of we-ness. However, Sam's family of origin, his sister in particular, was a source of support: Once or twice a week, when Sara worked the evening shift, she cooked dinner for Julia and Gabriel. Now and then, she also engaged the children in leisure activities (e.g., movies, picnics in the park) and attended Julia's school activities. The family's social network map (see Figure 4.1) revealed that their next-door neighbors; their pastor; Sara's mother, Diana; and her colleagues at the community hospital were people they trusted when they needed help. Diana bought groceries for the family and helped with household tasks.

Predisposing Factors

Chapter 3 discussed the individual, relational, and environmental factors that are linked to juvenile delinquency and criminal conduct. At the community level, three major conditions influenced Sam's and Gabriel's justice involvement: (a) neighborhood and school violence, (b) antisocial peer influence, and (c) social stigma. In the family, conflict, low cohesion, inconsistent monitoring, parental stress, and parental substance use represented criminogenic risks. At the individual level, Gabriel's emotional disturbance, poor academic performance, and lack of prosocial activities increased the likelihood of problem behaviors, including underage drinking and illicit marijuana use. Gabriel's scores on the YAS and the SDQ (self-report) provided additional evidence that family conflict, intrapersonal distress, a low ability to manage anger appropriately, and the absence of prosocial peers and occupations are significant concerns. His high level of emotional distress on the SDQ indicated a persistent pattern of worrying. His responses to individual

SDQ items also suggested difficulties with emotion regulation (i.e., "I get very angry and often lose my temper"). Sara's scores on the parent version of the SDQ represented her perception of Gabriel's functioning. Her report highlighted slightly elevated conduct problems (i.e., lies, loses his temper, seldom does what adults request). The results of the YAS also identified areas of strengths and barriers to prosocial conduct. Gabriel valued his family relationships and his bond with his father, mother, paternal aunt, and maternal grandmother. He was able to understand the consequences of risky behaviors; however, he did not know how to manage negative peer influence. He had doubts about the school system and whether his teachers could help him improve his grades and graduate from high school. According to Sara, Gabriel's individualized education program (IEP) had not been effective in addressing his learning difficulties. Sara showed interest in helping Gabriel out of the justice system and was supportive of his education; she hoped he would obtain his high school degree and go to the local community college. Sara indicated she stopped drinking when Gabriel was arrested. Julia's scores on the SDQ were within the normal range.

Precipitating Factors or Identifiable Stressors

Gabriel's arrest was the main event that had brought the family into treatment. Other precipitating factors that led to declines in individual and relational functioning include Sam's detention and subsequent family disruption and parenting stress. Incarceration is a situation of ambiguous loss and a stressor that creates uncertainty about family membership and family roles (Arditti, 2016; Boss, 2016). Sam was both physically absent and psychologically present; he was neither in nor out of the family system. Sara, Gabriel, and Julia had regular contact with Sam; however, Sam no longer participated in their everyday lives, and it was not clear whether and when he would come home. Uncertainty can undermine hope and generate feelings of helplessness; it can also produce anxiety. Sam's incarceration is a type of loss that is paradoxical and confusing because it is ongoing and has no closure. Uncertainty and confusion had immobilized the family and prevented them from adjusting to their new circumstances by reorganizing their relationships (Boss, 1999). Sara, Julia, and Gabriel felt isolated in their experience of loss; there were no social rituals to validate their emotions and walk them through grief. In addition, the stigma associated with imprisonment kept them from discussing their loss with others. As they grappled with Sam's absence on their own, they progressively withdrew from one another.

Perpetuating Factors

From a systemic perspective, problems occur in relational contexts, and the characteristics of these relational contexts—specifically, the interpersonal processes that prevent individuals and families from managing and resolving their difficulties successfully—are the focus of clinical attention. Figure 4.2 depicts the interaction patterns in the family that are thought to maintain

FIGURE 4.2. Relational Perpetuating Factors in the Family

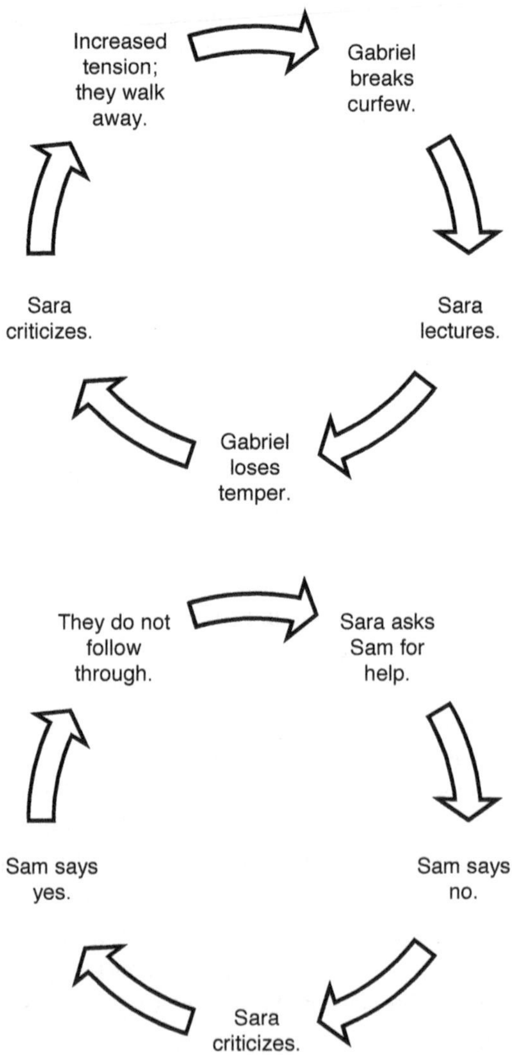

their distress. When Gabriel broke curfew, Sara would lecture him on the consequences of his actions. She would also criticize Gabriel for acting like his father. Gabriel would respond with anger, yell back at his mother, and bang doors. When Gabriel lost his temper, Sara would remind him to respect his elders. Negativity and conflict escalated until one of them walked away. Sara and Gabriel were stuck in problematic parent–child interactions characterized by low levels of warmth and trust as well as deficits in communication, problem solving, and conflict management. Sara had limited influence on Gabriel's behaviors. She would sometimes ask Sam to talk with his son; however, Sam was hesitant to discipline Gabriel. He was careful to use family visits and phone calls to maintain a positive relationship with his children, which increased Sara's resentment and parenting stress and led to arguments. Sara would describe Sam as unreliable and irresponsible and would threaten to end the family visits. To appease Sara, Sam would agree to speak to Gabriel in person. Neither Sara nor Sam followed through, and their negative exchanges increased relationship discord and mistrust.

Past Treatment

This was the first time the family received psychological services together, with the exception of Gabriel's testing and Sara's participation in her son's IEP team at school. Gabriel's IEP included special education services and accommodations: He was given extra time to complete his tests and assignments; he worked in small groups and with a peer tutor; and his teachers gave him copies of their lecture notes. Gabriel enjoyed meeting with the peer tutor and responded well to one-on-one support in the classroom. He also performed well in small groups. Despite the extra time, he was chronically late in submitting his homework assignments. In addition, he reported he did not understand the teachers' notes. Neither Sara nor Julia had participated in mental health treatment in the past. According to Sara, Sam's parole requirements involved alcohol and drug counseling; Sam also attended Narcotics Anonymous and Alcoholics Anonymous meetings. While in treatment, Sam relapsed many times.

IMPLICATIONS FOR CLINICAL INTERVENTION

The case formulation highlights several areas of intervention. At the individual level, Gabriel's emotional distress requires clinical attention. At the relational level, conflict and communication are processes that prevent the family from creating and maintaining emotional connection and cohesion; they undermine safety and trust and interfere with the exchange of information and support. For example, they keep Gabriel and Julia from discussing their experience of loss and thus limit Sara's ability to respond to her children's emotional needs. Parent–child conflict and poor communication also limit Sara's ability to monitor her children and teach them how to manage peer influence and other risk factors in their environment. Last, the family does not have clear and consistent strategies to address and solve concerns of everyday life in ways that allow Gabriel and Julia to exercise greater autonomy, participate in making decisions and setting limits, and develop competence and self-efficacy. At the contextual level, the family's social network is a resource that could be used to address gaps in adult monitoring and prosocial leisure activities. It is also important to focus on school–family communication about Gabriel's IEP to enhance his academic performance.

Assessment prepares the stage for clinical intervention. It involves creating conditions that facilitate therapeutic change—namely, engagement, emotional connection, a shared sense of purpose, and feelings of safety. It also involves gathering pertinent information about the clinical problem from different perspectives and sources using various methods. Case conceptualization is the process of organizing and interpreting assessment data to formulate an understanding of the family and the problem. The formulation of the problem precedes and validates clinical decisions about the type of treatment, the delivery format, and the therapeutic goals and in-session activities. Clinical decisions also integrate empirical knowledge of what works for specific problems and populations. This is the focus of the next chapter, Chapter 5, which presents information about family-focused intervention programs specifically designed for the prevention of violence and delinquency, in preparation for treatment planning, the topic of Chapter 6.

5 CLINICAL PRACTICE WITH JUSTICE-INVOLVED COUPLES AND FAMILIES

Evidence-Based Treatment Programs

Quality mental health care depends on practitioners' ability to make clinical decisions that integrate assessment data with scientific knowledge about specific clinical problems, diverse patient populations, and therapeutic interventions (APA Presidential Task Force on Evidence-Based Practice, 2006). Advanced knowledge of evidence-based couples and family treatment programs is also an essential component of professional competency in clinical practice with couples and families (Stanton & Welsh, 2011). This chapter presents current information about effective couples and family interventions that have been tested with justice-involved populations, namely, brief strategic family therapy (BSFT), functional family therapy (FFT), multidimensional family therapy (MDFT), multisystemic therapy (MST), and Treatment Foster Care Oregon (TFCO). FFT, MST, and TFCO are recognized as "model" approaches to juvenile delinquency by the National Institute of Justice (n.d.-a) and the Blueprints project at the University of Colorado Boulder (Blueprints for Healthy Youth Development, n.d.). BSFT, FFT, MDFT, MST, and TFCO are based on a large body of research, including randomized controlled trials in community settings, that has found positive treatment

https://doi.org/10.1037/0000285-006
Best Clinical Practices for Treating Families in Juvenile and Criminal Justice Systems, by C. C. Datchi

outcomes for adolescent conduct problems and substance use (e.g., Baldwin et al., 2012). Couples- and family-based treatment for adult correctional populations is still in the early stage of development (Datchi, Barretti, & Thompson, 2016; Datchi & Sexton, 2016). FFT, the Prevention and Relationship Enhancement Program (PREP; Einhorn et al., 2008), the Creating Lasting Family Connections Marriage Enhancement Program (CLFCMEP; Shamblen et al., 2013), the Strengthening Families Program (SFP; A. L. Miller et al., 2013), and Community Reinforcement and Family Training (CRAFT; J. M. Miller et al., 2016) are some of the few evidence-based interventions that have been adapted for adults in the criminal justice system.

This chapter describes the programs just listed and discusses recent family-focused innovations in the treatment of justice-involved populations. Information is provided to answer five specific questions about effective couples- and family-based programs: What are (a) the demographics of the target populations, (b) the types of clinical problems, (c) the treatment goals and (d) desired outcomes, and (e) the theoretical mechanisms that lead to therapeutic change? This information is intended to support clinical decisions about services and activities that are most likely to produce positive outcomes in the context of the client's characteristics (e.g., social identities, personality traits, symptoms, life cycle) and preferences (e.g., beliefs, goals; APA Presidential Task Force on Evidence-Based Practice, 2006). The chapter begins with a summary of the empirical evidence supporting the effectiveness of couples- and family-based programs with juvenile and adult offenders. The information stems from major research reviews, meta-analyses, and individual studies published since 2010. The discussion does not include research on parenting programs that focus on the prevention of conduct problems early in the family life cycle. (For recent findings on the effectiveness of parent training, see Sexton et al., 2013, and Piquero et al., 2016.) Although parenting interventions are family focused, they are directed at young children's externalizing behaviors; their goals are to increase parents' capacity to manage problem behaviors and promote positive youth development and improve parent–child interactions and parental supervision and thus minimize the risk of future contact with the justice system.

EFFECTIVENESS OF COUPLES- AND FAMILY-BASED INTERVENTIONS FOR JUVENILE AND ADULT OFFENDERS

Family therapy is recognized as the treatment of choice for antisocial conduct in adolescence (Datchi & Sexton, 2016). Systematic reviews of family therapy research have shown that the findings, for the most part, support the effectiveness of family-focused interventions for juvenile delinquency (Sexton et al., 2013). The mean effect sizes of family therapy programs such as MST and FFT are $d = 0.26$ for effectiveness studies conducted in community-based agencies and $d = 0.81$ for efficacy studies conducted in university clinics under controlled conditions (Baldwin et al., 2012; Sexton et al., 2013). These effect sizes correspond to 63% and 90.5% success rates for youth externalizing behaviors (e.g., aggression, delinquency). The difference in magnitude of effect between efficacy and effectiveness research speaks to the complexity of transporting evidence-based treatment models from academic settings to the real world (Henggeler & Sheidow, 2012). On average, this process lasts 1 to 2 years and requires considerable training, consultation, and evaluation of staff performance and model adherence (see https://www.tfcoregon.com/, and MDFT, n.d.).

Studies of couples therapy have evaluated primarily the effects of treatment on global relationship satisfaction (Carr, 2019; Rathgeber et al., 2019; Roddy et al., 2020). The most well-researched models are behavioral couples therapy and emotionally focused couples therapy. Randomized controlled trials have shown that behavioral couples therapy and emotionally focused couples therapy were superior to wait list control groups, with medium to small effect sizes at termination and a 6-month follow-up (Rathgeber et al., 2019). Roddy and colleagues (2020) looked at the impact of various couples therapy approaches and reported large to moderate effects of treatment on relationship satisfaction and communication. For the most part, knowledge about couples therapy is based on samples of married, heterosexual, White partners with an average age of 38 years and an average relationship length of 9 years. To date, there has been no rigorous investigation of couples therapy with criminal justice populations in the United States, except as they related to intimate partner violence. A meta-analytic review of intimate partner violence studies indicated that couples therapy was marginally more effective than individual-based interventions in reducing situational couple violence (Karakurt et al., 2016). Again, the studies involved a majority of White couples (70%) with an average age of 34 years. Future research is needed to determine whether couples therapy can enhance protective processes in racially and ethnically diverse couple relationships to prevent and reduce criminal conduct and recidivism.

The next sections review the findings of recent meta-analyses and cost-effectiveness studies of family therapy for adolescent conduct problems. The review shows that there is continuing support for the clinical and economic utility of systemic interventions with juvenile justice populations. At present, there are only a few individual studies, and no published reports of meta-analysis and cost-effectiveness studies, of couple and family interventions for adults in the correctional system.

Meta-Analyses of Family Therapy

Many meta-analyses of family therapy studies have been conducted (e.g., Shadish et al., 1995; Shadish & Baldwin, 2003). Among the most recent are two publications on the effectiveness of several family-based treatments for juvenile delinquency (Baldwin et al., 2012; Dopp et al., 2017) and five meta-analyses of research on BSFT, FFT, MDFT, MST, and TFCO (Åström et al., 2020; Hartnett et al., 2017; Lindstrøm et al., 2015; van der Pol et al., 2017; van der Stouwe et al., 2014). Baldwin and colleagues (2012) reviewed 11 studies of BSFT, FFT, MDFT, and MST and found that effect sizes varied by type of comparison ($d = 0.70$ for family therapy vs. a control group and $d = 0.26$ for family therapy vs. alternative interventions). For delinquency and substance use, family therapy had larger effect sizes (*ds* = 0.31, 0.43) than alternative treatments. Dopp and colleagues (2017) found similar results confirming the superiority of family therapy programs (i.e., FFT, MST, and TFCO) to individual-focused services for severe delinquency. Their meta-analysis included 28 studies with an average effect size of $d = 0.24$. The effects of family therapy persisted up to 2.5 years after completion. Treatment had greater effects on adolescent substance use ($d = 0.41$), followed by school functioning ($d = 0.29$) and antisocial behaviors ($d = 0.25$). The findings also suggested that Hispanic youth and high-risk offenders experienced more benefits than their counterparts.

Meta-analyses of single programs provide additional support for the effectiveness of family therapy for adolescent conduct problems. Hartnett and colleagues (2017) estimated the effects of FFT compared with no treatment, treatment as usual, and well-defined alternative interventions. They separated the results by research design (i.e., random assignment or not) and found that FFT produced better outcomes compared to no treatment and alternative interventions in both types of investigations. The pooled effect sizes were significant and ranged from $d = 0.35$ to $d = 0.90$. A meta-analysis of 22 studies revealed significant small effects of MST on measures of general delinquency ($d = 0.23$), parental mental health ($d = 0.32$), and parenting ($d = 0.14$) for juvenile offenders under age 15 (van der Stouwe et al., 2014). The effects of MST increased in magnitude when the research samples were predominantly White with a history of prior arrests and when MST was compared with a single, nonmultimodal program. The findings also suggested that treatment duration and completion moderated the impact of MST on delinquency outcomes. Likewise, a meta-analysis of 18 studies showed that TFCO reduced youth risk of recidivism (Åström et al., 2020): The treatment effects on delinquency were statistically significant and small to moderate depending on the source of the information (i.e., $d = 0.24$ for self-report and $d = 0.39$ for police and court records). The results also suggested that TFCO had little impact on youth substance use and association with antisocial peers. Van der Pol and colleagues (2017) reviewed 19 studies that compared MDFT with individual cognitive behavior therapy, group therapy, and combined therapy. Their findings showed that MDFT was superior to alternative interventions for the treatment of adolescents with moderate to severe substance abuse and disruptive behavior problems ($d = 0.28$ for moderate substance abuse and 0.38 for severe substance abuse). There were no differences in outcomes for male and female youth and various racial and ethnic groups. At this time, there is limited evidence that BSFT is an effective intervention for adolescent conduct problems and substance use: The results of a meta-analysis including three randomized controlled trials showed that BSFT was more successful in engaging and retaining youth and families compared with alternative interventions; however, there were no significant differences in reduction of drug use and family functioning between BSFT and other programs (Lindstrøm et al., 2015).

Few studies have compared the outcomes of evidence-based family therapy programs. Baglivio, Jackowski, et al. (2014) evaluated the relative effectiveness of MST and FFT in a sample of adolescents under the supervision of the Florida Department of Juvenile Justice. After controlling for selection bias, they found that youth who participated in FFT were less likely to recidivate during treatment compared with youth in MST. In particular, there were significant between-group differences for female offenders, with about 38% of new arrests and probation violations in MST and 26% in FFT. Likewise, 32% of low-risk juvenile offenders committed a new offense during MST services compared with 21% in FFT. The results for moderate-high to high-risk youth were mixed; however, they showed that recidivism rates were higher in MST (41%) than FFT (31.7%).

Cost-Effectiveness of Evidence-Based Family Therapy Programs

Benefit–cost analyses suggest that evidence-based family therapy programs for juvenile delinquency achieve desired outcomes that offset the costs of service delivery. In Washington State, FFT, MST, and TFCO offered a return on investment that ranged from $18.75 (FFT for youth after release) to $4.29 (TFCO for court-involved youth) and $3.02 (MST for court-involved youth after release; Washington State Institute for Public Policy, 2019). A systematic review of cost-effectiveness studies found that FFT was superior to a skill-training group intervention for substance use disorders and delinquency up to 12 months after treatment. MST was cost-effective for the treatment of juvenile sex offenses and severe delinquency, but not for the treatment of adolescent conduct disorders (Goorden, Schawo, et al., 2016; Klietz et al., 2010). A study conducted in Europe found that the overall costs of MST were 50% lower than the control condition, which consisted of family therapy, community supervision, and other supportive interventions; there were no significant differences in the effects of treatment on antisocial and violent behaviors (Vermeulen et al., 2017). The research also suggests that MDFT produces better outcomes than individual cognitive behavior therapy for adolescents with cannabis use disorders (Goorden, van der Schee, et al., 2016). When one takes into consideration the costs of delinquency associated with substance use, one sees that MDFT is not significantly more expensive than individual cognitive behavior therapy. Likewise, a cost–benefit analysis of TFCO compared with a group care program showed long-term positive effects on arrest, conviction, and incarceration with a return on investment that increased by 400% at a 10-year follow-up (Saldana et al., 2019). The sample was composed of young women who had received services in adolescence, and the findings indicated that TFCO reduced the likelihood of justice involvement in adulthood.

EVIDENCE-BASED FAMILY THERAPY PROGRAMS FOR JUVENILE OFFENDERS

Systematic reviews and meta-analyses provide valuable information about best practices in the treatment of adolescent delinquency. In particular, they highlight the psychological, social, and economic benefits of four family intervention programs for juvenile offenders: (a) FFT, (b) MDFT, (c) MST, and (d) TFCO. Although research on BSFT has produced inconsistent findings, recent studies indicate that BSFT is an effective intervention when clinicians deliver services with fidelity to the treatment manual (Horigian, Feaster, Brincks, et al., 2015; Horigian, Feaster, Robbins, et al., 2015). This section gives an overview of each program and their underpinning theory as well as target populations, clinical problems, and goals. It also includes a summary of current empirical knowledge about their outcomes and mechanisms of change.

Brief Strategic Family Therapy

BSFT is a manualized family therapy program originally designed to address the unique concerns of Cuban immigrant youth with substance use and behavior problems (Szapocznik et al., 2016). The BSFT model is a present- and problem-focused integrative one that combines concepts and techniques from structural and strategic family therapy, two treatment approaches developed in the 1960s by Salvador Minuchin and Jay Haley, respectively. Since its inception in the mid-1970s, BSFT has been implemented and tested with Hispanic, Black, and White American youth and their families. BSFT is intended to be short in duration, between 12 and 16 family sessions delivered in community-based mental health clinics, drug treatment programs, and families' homes (Lindstrøm et al., 2015).

Core Concepts

The BSFT model defines the family as a system that consists of interdependent individuals interacting with each other in repetitive patterns (Szapocznik et al., 2016). These interaction patterns constitute the family structure and determine the family's ability to resolve difficulties and meet their needs and goals. They are assessed on six dimensions: (a) organization (i.e., leadership or hierarchy, subsystem membership and cross-generational coalitions, boundaries, triangulation, communication), (b) resonance (i.e., psychological and emotional closeness between family members), (c) developmental stages and transitions, (d) life or social context (e.g., extended family, community), (e) identified client, and (f) conflict resolution. Interaction patterns are deemed maladaptive when they maintain individual symptoms.

Treatment Goals

BSFT aims to reduce adolescent drug use and behavior problems by changing the family's maladaptive patterns that are directly related to the youth's antisocial conduct and by developing or strengthening interactions that support optimal individual and family functioning. In particular, BSFT targets family dynamics that have been shown to predict adolescent drug use and externalizing behaviors (e.g., poor parental monitoring and parent–youth communication; Szapocznik et al., 2003; also see Chapter 3, this volume).

Therapeutic Process

BSFT consists of five stages, or steps, with specific interventions (Lindstrøm et al., 2015; Szapocznik et al., 2016). The first step corresponds to the formation of the therapeutic system and the development of the therapeutic alliances through the use of *joining techniques*: In Step 1, BSFT therapists join or become a part of the family system by communicating empathy with, respect for, and acceptance of the family structure and organization. In particular, they support the family members who have the most influence to keep the family in treatment and recognize the clinician's leadership role (Szapocznik et al., 2003). They also observe and mirror the family's style of behaving and speaking so as to blend with them. In Steps 2 and 3, BSFT therapists specify the concerns for which the family is seeking treatment and identify the adaptive and maladaptive interactions that are most relevant to the presenting problems. They use the *tracking* technique to diagnose repetitive family patterns: They encourage family members to interact with one another as they typically do at home and observe their behavioral exchanges to make inferences about their habitual transactions. In the initial sessions, BSFT therapists also target the family's negative affect and aim to increase their motivation for change (Step 4). They use the technique of *reframing* to foster different perspectives, reduce blame, and prepare the family for restructuring (Step 5). *Restructuring* involves shifting boundaries and alliances to establish parents' leadership and increase their ability to manage and influence their child's behaviors. It also involves learning new skills (e.g., conflict resolution, effective parenting) to develop new adaptive interaction patterns.

Treatment Outcomes

Research has highlighted the positive effects of BSFT on diverse outcomes: family functioning, adolescent conduct problems, association with antisocial peers, youth marijuana and alcohol use, and parental alcohol use (Horigian, Feaster, Brincks, et al., 2015; Horigian, Feaster, Robbins, et al., 2015; Robbins et al., 2011; Szapocznik et al., 2015; Valdez et al., 2013).

Family Functioning. BSFT has been found to be more efficacious than individual psychodynamic and group therapy in improving family functioning up to 1 year after intervention, when measured by independent raters (Szapocznik et al., 2015). Although families improved during BSFT, they showed significant signs of deterioration in the alternative treatment conditions. The positive outcomes of BSFT were greater for Hispanic families relative to Black families. Research in community settings suggests there may be discrepancies in perceptions of family functioning (Robbins et al., 2011): Parents in BSFT reported statistically significant improvements compared with treatment as usual; adolescents did not. In addition, BSFT had positive effects on parental functioning, mediated by parents' perception of family functioning.

Substance Use. Current evidence suggests that BSFT reduces youth level of drug and alcohol use; however, more research is needed to establish BSFT as an effective approach to adolescent substance use problems. A randomized controlled trial showed that youth in BSFT reported fewer days of drug use than the comparison group at a 12-month follow-up (Robbins et al., 2011). There were no treatment differences in the proportion of positive drug tests. Valdez and colleagues (2013) evaluated the relative effectiveness of BSFT with gang-affiliated Mexican American adolescents ages 12 to 17. The study participants received an enhanced version of BSFT that included four additional components. Compared with the alternative treatment, BSFT produced greater reductions in the frequency of alcohol use within the past month. For marijuana use, BSFT was not superior to treatment as usual. Horigian, Feaster, Robbins, and colleagues (2015) reported similar results regarding adolescent drug use. They investigated the long-term impact of BSFT from adolescence to young adulthood and found an increase in the number of drug use days from baseline to follow-up, from 2.5 to 12.1 for the BSFT group and from 2.8 to 13.8 for the comparison group. Therapists' model adherence was linked to treatment outcomes: Clinicians who achieved high levels of joining throughout treatment and who used restructuring interventions were more effective in reducing adolescent drug use (Szapocznik et al., 2015). Treatment retention was also linked to lower levels of drug use. Horigian, Feaster, Brincks, and colleagues (2015) found that BSFT produced greater reductions in parental alcohol use than treatment as usual.

Delinquency. Research has shown that BSFT is superior to group therapy in decreasing adolescent conduct problems and association with antisocial peers (Szapocznik et al., 2015; Valdez et al., 2013). Parental reports in one study indicated that BSFT produced statistically significant reductions in youth conduct problems, impulsivity, and hyperactivity at a 6-month follow-up, with moderate to strong effect sizes ranging from $d = 0.52$ to $d = 0.61$ (Valdez et al., 2013). Youth who had participated in BSFT were less likely to display externalizing behavior problems in young adulthood compared with those who received treatment as usual; they were also less likely to be arrested and incarcerated (Horigian, Feaster, Robbins, et al., 2015).

Functional Family Therapy

FFT is a family-based intervention program designed for the treatment of adolescent delinquency. Since its development in the 1970s, FFT has been used with diverse communities in the United States, Europe, and Australia and has been tested with low- and high-risk juvenile offenders (Henggeler &

Sheidow, 2012; Sexton, 2016). The program is delivered in the family's home or in community-based settings, including schools, probation offices, and mental health clinics. On average, treatment lasts 4 to 6 months, depending on the severity of the problems.

Core Concepts

FFT is defined by a set of systemic principles that inform therapists' understanding of adolescent behaviors as they occur in the context of interactions within and between the family and other systems, such as the school and the community (Sexton, 2011, 2016). The focus of treatment is the relational processes that prevent the family from working together and performing critical functions during adolescence: maintaining parental involvement and emotional support, protecting youth from various risk factors, and allowing them to exercise independence. It is the combination of, and balance between, risk and protective factors in the individual, the family, and the environment that determine the likelihood of delinquent behaviors. FFT clinicians assess how those factors influence the family's attempts to solve problems; in particular, they evaluate the interaction patterns that have developed from the family's efforts to manage the youth's conduct. Patterns that are ineffective and maladaptive are a primary target of interventions. FFT also emphasizes the principle of matching treatment to families' characteristics and relational functions in particular. The FFT concept of *relational functions* refers to the level of relational connection and relational power between individuals in the family system.

Treatment Goals

The FFT model is designed to treat youth risky behaviors and thus prevent and reduce juvenile delinquency and justice involvement (i.e., reoffending, rearrest, incarceration, placement out of the home; Weisman & Montgomery, 2019). FFT aims to produce behavioral change that is attainable and relevant to families' presenting concerns, values, and preferences (Sexton, 2016). The goals are to disrupt maladaptive family processes and replace them with new relational patterns that will enhance the family's success at managing youth conduct problems.

Therapeutic Process

The clinical protocol of FFT guides the implementation of the model in three successive and continuous phases: (a) engagement and motivation, (b) behavior change, and (c) generalization (Sexton, 2011). Each phase is characterized by specific goals, activities, and outcomes. In the *engagement and motivation* phase, FFT clinicians seek to reduce blame and negativity in family interactions, to develop a balanced alliance, and to agree on a relational definition of the problem. Reframing is a core intervention of the FFT model; it is used to instill hope, engage the family in the therapeutic process, increase their motivation to try new solutions, and create a shared sense of purpose. In *behavior change*, therapists aim to build the family's competencies by teaching skills (e.g., clear and direct communication, problem solving) that will foster the development of protective processes and act as a buffer against risks. In *generalization*, the goal is to maintain change and promote a sense of mastery by supporting families' efforts to use new skills in various situations. This may require connecting the family to relevant community resources and guiding the family in their interactions with other systems.

Treatment Outcomes

FFT has been tested with racially and ethnically diverse populations as well as male and female youth. There is evidence that families who receive FFT services experience improvements in their everyday life and relationships and that FFT reduces adolescent externalizing behaviors (e.g., aggression), reoffending, and substance use.

Family Functioning. Research indicates that FFT produces positive changes in family functioning and parenting from baseline to termination and follow-up (Celinska et al., 2019; Vardanian et al., 2020; White et al., 2013). In particular, families who participate in FFT experience increased stability at home and parental involvement (White et al., 2013) and display higher levels of engagement than comparison groups (Henggeler & Sheidow, 2012). Vardanian and colleagues (2020) reported small to moderate effects of FFT on parent and youth perceived quality of family life; however, FFT was not found to perform better than the alternative treatment in a predominantly White and Black U.S. sample of juvenile offenders under family court supervision (Celinska et al., 2019) and in a sample of White youth in England (Humayun et al., 2017).

Substance Use. Research has yielded inconsistent results for youth substance use outcomes. The results have shown that FFT had a positive, short-term impact on adolescent marijuana use that lasted 3 months after the end of treatment (Henggeler & Sheidow, 2012). Systematic reviews also suggest that the effects of FFT on adolescent substance use are not statistically significant (Weisman & Montgomery, 2019).

Delinquency. There is strong evidence that FFT decreases the likelihood of juvenile recidivism when implemented with fidelity to the treatment model (Celinska et al., 2019; Sexton & Turner, 2010). Randomized controlled trials have shown that FFT reduced felony and violent crimes by more than 30% (Sexton & Turner, 2010); it also reduced the odds of out-of-home placement, technical violations, and convictions for new drug and property offenses by 75%, 66.9%, 98.7%, and 92.7%, respectively (Celinska et al., 2019; Darnell & Schuler, 2015). High levels of treatment adherence were associated with better outcomes: In FFT, the average rate of youth reoffending was 14.5% compared with 22% for youth receiving probation services (Sexton & Turner, 2010). This difference was statistically significant. In the Netherlands, FFT was compared with MST and found to be equally as beneficial (Eeren et al., 2018). However, adolescents who participated in MST displayed lower levels of externalizing behavior problems and greater engagement in school and work after treatment. Gottfredson and colleagues (2018) evaluated an adaptation of FFT for gang-involved youth with a sample that was predominantly Black and male. They found that FFT youth had lower rates of adjudication and drug and property charges at an 18-month follow-up, compared with treatment as usual. Parental substance use, residential instability, and youth school problems are factors that moderate the success of FFT (Limoncelli et al., 2019). In particular, they constitute barriers to participation and are associated with a greater number of missed therapy sessions. Parental substance use is also related to a higher odds of premature termination. In sum, FFT is an effective intervention program for juvenile delinquency and violence; it has produced benefits that exceeds the costs, and the rate of return on investment is 641% (Gottfredson et al., 2018; S. Lee et al., 2012).

Multidimensional Family Therapy

MDFT is an evidence-based, integrative therapy program for adolescents with substance use and conduct problems (Liddle, 2016; Rowe, 2010). It is a multidimensional treatment that intervenes at several levels: individual (youth and parent), relational (parent–youth and family relationships), and mesosystemic (the family's interactions with external systems, e.g., the school). The theoretical framework of MDFT combines knowledge about the determinants of adolescent externalizing behaviors, dynamic systems theory, and developmental and ecological principles of human functioning over the life course. MDFT has been implemented in the United States, Canada, and Europe with racially diverse populations of youth ages 11 to 18 (Rowe, 2010). The duration and frequency of treatment range from 3 to 6 months and one to several sessions per week. Detention to Community is an adaptation of the MDFT program for incarcerated youth (Liddle, 2014; Liddle et al., 2011). During detention, adolescents and their families participate in activities designed to promote family involvement, facilitate reentry, and reduce youth risk of contracting HIV or a sexually transmitted disease. The Detention to Community adaptation also emphasizes the development of collaborative cross-system partnerships between clinicians and juvenile justice personnel to support youth compliance with legal requirements.

Core Concepts

MDFT defines individuals and families as *holons*, a term that describes the holistic nature of each and their interconnectedness (Liddle, 2016). A person is a system with parts that work together as one; they are also part of the family and other social systems. Each holon is a focus of assessment and a site of intervention. Their relation and interactions with each other are critical areas of clinical attention. The concept of holon highlights the multidimensional factors that influence adolescent behaviors, which include youth biology, personality, and ecology. MDFT targets those individual, familial, and environmental factors that are known to contribute to adolescent substance use and related conduct problems. Family functioning is of particular importance because of its primary influence on youth positive development.

Treatment Goals

The primary goals of MDFT are to reduce and prevent adolescent substance use and delinquency (Multidimensional Family Therapy, n.d.). The secondary objectives are to improve individual and relational outcomes for youth and their parents in the areas of mental health, family relationships, and school- and work-related behaviors. In particular, MDFT aims to increase youth self-awareness, self-worth, and confidence; their ability to use emotion regulation, decision making, communication, and problem-solving skills effectively; and their participation in prosocial activities with peers (Multidimensional Family Therapy, n.d.). MDFT also fosters family and parenting competence through psychoeducation, skill building, and coaching (Liddle, 2016). It seeks to repair and strengthen the emotional bonds that connect family members; it also aims to improve the family's interactions with other social systems (e.g., school, juvenile justice) and their capacity to access and use external resources.

Therapeutic Process

Treatment involves individual sessions with youth and their parents separately; family sessions; and interactions with other social systems, such as the school (Liddle, 2016). Services are delivered in three continuous phases. In the first phase, clinicians set the stage for change and create conditions that promote the development of strong therapeutic relationships with the youth, the parents, and the family. In particular, they demonstrate compassion and respect while working collaboratively with the family members to develop a shared understanding of the problem and agree on the focus of therapy sessions. Clinicians gather information about the youth, the parents, and the family environment, giving special attention to developmental challenges and ecological factors, including parenting practices, health, and relationship difficulties. In individual sessions with youth and parents, they facilitate conversations to assess the nature and severity of the problems, stimulate self-reflection and engagement, enhance emotional connection, and increase hope and motivation to participate in treatment. From these conversations, clinicians extract themes that translate into behavior change goals with relevant skill training components. In Phases 2 and 3, therapists work with family members, individually and together, to build and support new behavioral competencies and positive interaction patterns that enable the family to successfully address the youth's drug use, resolve family conflict, and negotiate with other social systems. In addition, clinicians work with the youth's school to address behavior problems. In MDFT, assessment is ongoing and calls for the constant evaluation of therapeutic interventions and their effects on individual and familial outcomes. It also includes drug testing the adolescent in individual sessions.

Treatment Outcomes

There is strong evidence that MDFT has positive effects on adolescent conduct and substance use problems. Randomized controlled trials have shown that MDFT produced significant reductions in delinquency and drug use that persisted up to 3 years after treatment (Dakof et al., 2015; Liddle et al., 2018; van der Pol, Henderson, et al., 2018; van der Pol, Hendriks, et al., 2018). MDFT has been evaluated in various settings (e.g., community and university-based clinics, juvenile drug court, juvenile detention) with diverse populations (e.g., White, Black, Hispanic, and Western European male and female adolescents).

Family Functioning. Past research reported that MDFT had a positive effect on family functioning and family conflict and cohesion specifically (Liddle et al., 2001). Studies published after 2010 do not include further information about this treatment outcome.

Substance Use. MDFT was found to lower the frequency of substance use by 76% from intake to a 6-month follow-up for a sample of youth in juvenile drug court (Dakof et al., 2015). The findings indicated that MDFT and cognitive behavior group therapy produced similar outcomes, and adolescents who participated in both types of treatment maintained lower levels of substance use compared with baseline, after being discharged from drug court. Likewise, youth who received MDFT in the community reported significant decreases in substance use problems and fared as well as their counterparts in residential treatment (Liddle et al., 2018). The effects of both MDFT and residential treatment were large for frequency of substance use, with reductions of 80% and more during the first 2 months of therapy. At an 18-month follow-up, youth in MDFT reported less increase in substance use problems than youth in residential treatment.

Delinquency. The evidence suggests that MDFT produces reductions in delinquency that last up to 3 years after the start of treatment (Dakof et al., 2015; Liddle et al., 2011, 2018; van der Pol, Henderson, et al., 2018; van der Pol, Hendriks, et al., 2018). Research has shown that youth who participated in MDFT were less likely to commit serious crimes than peers who received cognitive behavior therapy (Dakof et al., 2015); in fact, they maintained lower levels of conduct problems from baseline to a 2-year follow-up, with a decrease of 26% in serious crimes, whereas their counterparts reported a 33% increase in severe delinquent behaviors. Likewise, MDFT was found to be superior to residential treatment in the long term: Youth in MDFT experienced the benefits of the program up to 18 months after intake, whereas adolescents in residential treatment reported an increased frequency of delinquent behaviors (Liddle et al., 2018). Studies of MDFT have confirmed the positive and long-term effects of MDFT with European samples of juvenile offenders (van der Pol, Henderson, et al., 2018; van der Pol, Hendriks, et al., 2018): Arrest rates, number of offenses, and severity of crimes declined after the start of treatment; the severity and number of crimes reached levels of almost zero 3 years after treatment. These findings suggest that adolescent behavior outcomes are similar in MDFT and individual cognitive behavior therapy.

Multisystemic Family Therapy

MST is an evidence-based, short-term, intensive intervention program for high-risk juvenile offenders (Henggeler & Schaeffer, 2016; Schoenwald et al., 2016). It integrates the tenets of various theories—social ecological, social learning, family systems, and strategic—into a set of treatment principles that guide clinical decisions and actions. MST targets the multiple risk factors that are associated with delinquency. Services are individually tailored to the characteristics and needs of clients and are delivered in the youth's home, school, neighborhood, and/or community, where the behavior problems occur, over the span of 3 to 5 months. The MST model has been adapted to treat juvenile sex offenders and youth with comorbid substance use and conduct problems.

Core Concepts

MST stresses the reciprocal influence between an individual and their social ecology (Henggeler & Schaeffer, 2016; Henggeler & Sheidow, 2012). Delinquency is understood in the context of the youth's interactions within the family and with the school, the neighborhood, and the juvenile justice system, where risk factors determine the likelihood of offending. MST also emphasizes the strengths and resources of individuals, families, and communities. Strengths are viewed as levers for change.

Treatment Goals

MST aims to change the primary conditions that influence adolescent conduct problems, including transactions between individuals and between systems. The goal is to create an environment that promotes adaptive behaviors at home and in the community (e.g., relationships with prosocial peers, improved school performance, effective and developmentally appropriate parenting; Henggeler & Schaeffer, 2016; Henggeler & Sheidow, 2012). MST seeks to increase parental competencies and empower caregivers to protect youth against multiple risk factors as well as to secure the help of relatives, friends, and community members to support change and maintain treatment gains (e.g., a neighbor helps to monitor the youth after school).

Therapeutic Process

MST is present focused, and interventions are selected to resolve specific behavior problems (Henggeler & Schaeffer, 2016). The therapeutic process is collaborative and involves the clinicians, the family, and key stakeholders such as teachers and justice officials. It starts with a discussion that explores the desired outcomes and results in the specification of shared treatment goals. MST clinicians work with the youth, the family, and other important systems to assess the youth's ecology and formulate hypotheses about the determinants of the presenting problems. The case formulation guides the choice of therapeutic techniques; these are borrowed from empirically supported treatments such as cognitive behavior therapy and behavioral parent training with considerations for the youth's developmental needs. Outcome assessment is a critical component of the therapeutic process: Therapists gather information about the effectiveness of MST interventions from the perspectives of the adolescent, the caregivers, and other stakeholders. When treatment activities do not produce the desired outcomes, new hypotheses are developed and new techniques selected.

Treatment Outcomes

More than 30 years of research on the efficacy and effectiveness of MST has been conducted with racially and ethnically diverse juvenile offenders in the United States and Europe (Henggeler & Schaeffer, 2016). The findings indicate that MST improves family functioning and decreases juvenile recidivism, out-of-home placement, and substance use.

Family Functioning. MST was shown to improve caregivers' functioning, parenting skills, and family relationships (Blankestein et al., 2019; Deković et al., 2012; Johnides et al., 2017). Compared with treatment as usual, MST produced greater increases in perceived parental competence, positive discipline, and caregiver–youth relationship quality (Deković et al., 2012). Perceived parental competence predicted positive discipline, which in turn was linked to decreases in adolescent behavior problems. The evidence suggests that the therapeutic alliance between the caregiver and the therapist mediates the effects of MST on parenting; specifically, the strength of the emotional bond between the caregiver and the clinician was found to be associated with improved parental monitoring (Glebova et al., 2018). MST also has a beneficial impact on caregivers' functioning. A 20-year follow-up evaluation of MST showed that caregivers of high-risk juvenile offenders who participated in MST had lower odds of felony arrests compared with caregivers in individual therapy (Johnides et al., 2017); they were also less likely to be involved with the justice system for reasons related to family instability. In addition, the follow-up evaluation highlighted the mechanisms that mediated the effects of MST on caregivers: Increases in family cohesion and decreases in family conflict and defensive communication predicted lower rates of caregivers' contact with the criminal justice system.

Substance Use. MST was found to have positive effects on adolescents with comorbid substance use and severe conduct problems (Henggeler & Schaeffer, 2016). Reductions in substance use lasted up to 4 years after the end of treatment. These benefits generalized to the siblings of juvenile offenders who received MST services.

Delinquency. MST is a cost-effective intervention for the reduction and prevention of juvenile recidivism. Researchers have estimated that MST produced savings that ranged from $3 to $48 for every dollar invested in the program (Borduin & Dopp, 2015; Dopp et al., 2018; Klietz et al., 2010). Juvenile offenders who received MST services for problematic sexual behaviors were less likely to recidivate than their counterparts in group and individual therapy (Borduin & Dopp, 2015). The probability of being arrested for any crime during the 8-year follow-up period was 4 times higher in the comparison group. Likewise, a statewide implementation and evaluation of MST showed that the program produced significant reductions in monthly rates of juvenile offenses and court petitions from baseline to posttreatment (Dopp et al., 2018). MST also had long-term favorable effects on gang-involved youth (Boxer et al., 2017) and youth with antisocial behaviors and intellectual disability (Blankestein et al., 2019). It reduced the number of police contact, rates of offending and arrest, adolescent rule-breaking behaviors, school absences (Weiss et al., 2013), and out-of-home placement (Vidal et al., 2017). Treatment gains were maintained up to 21 years after treatment (A. M. Sawyer & Borduin, 2011).

Treatment Foster Care Oregon

TFCO is an evidence-based program for serious and chronic juvenile offenders age 12 to 18 years. Instead of detention or other residential facilities, youth are placed in a foster home where they participate in intensive individual and family services (Fisher & Gilliam, 2012; Henggeler & Sheidow, 2012). There are currently 35 TFCO sites in the United States and Europe (https://www.tfcoregon.com/), and services are delivered by a team of professionals, including family and individual therapists, skill trainers and coaches, and parenting consultants (Fisher & Gilliam, 2012).

Core Concepts

TFCO is based on the principles of social learning theory and empirical research on the correlates of adolescent antisocial behaviors (Fisher & Gilliam, 2012; J. Snyder & Stoolmiller, 2002). The assumption is that delinquency is the result of multiple processes that co-occur in different domains of the youth's ecology, including the family, the peer group, the school, and the community (Chamberlain, 2003). Behavior change takes place in the natural environment where the conduct problems develop and persist. In particular, parent–youth interactions and parenting practices are primary targets of TFCO interventions.

Treatment Goals

TFCO aims to promote the development of adolescent prosocial behaviors by enhancing caregivers' parenting skills and creating a family context that offers structure, consistent discipline, positive reinforcement, monitoring, and affection (Chamberlain, 2003). The objectives are to reduce exposure to antisocial peers, increase participation in prosocial activities, and enhance school performance.

Therapeutic Process

TFCO begins with the recruitment and training of foster parents in the use of behavioral management and reinforcement strategies (Fisher & Gilliam, 2012). Foster parents are integral members of the treatment team and key actors in the development and implementation of the youth's behavior program. When a youth is placed in a foster home, the TFCO team has daily contact with the foster parents to collect information about the youth's behaviors, identify behavior management targets, and assist with challenging situations and emergencies (Chamberlain, 2003; Fisher & Gilliam, 2012). The foster parents also participate in weekly group meetings, where they receive additional support from their peers. During the youth's foster care placement, the TFCO team provides consultation to foster parents and teachers; team members also attend school meetings to monitor and promote the youth's academic success. The youth's behavior management program consists of a system of rewards that is designed to encourage a cooperative attitude and positive activities (e.g., getting out of bed on time, attending classes, doing chores). Adolescents also learn problem solving and other prosocial skills with the help of a coach or therapist. Interventions are tailored to the developmental and mental health needs of the youth. The goal is to reunite the youth with the aftercare family (i.e., biological parents, adoptive parents, or relatives). Before reunification, the aftercare family works with a TFCO family therapist and learns how to implement effective parenting and behavior management strategies. Family therapy also involves training in communication, problem solving, and conflict management skills (Chamberlain, 2003).

Treatment Outcomes

Studies of TFCO have evaluated the effects of the program on serious juvenile offenders and shown that it reduced the rates of externalizing behavior symptoms, violent offenses, criminal charges, out-of-home placement, and incarceration (Bergström & Höjman, 2016; Fisher & Gilliam, 2012; Henggeler & Sheidow, 2012; Westermark et al., 2011). TFCO was found to be superior to traditional residential care and to produce positive outcomes that lasted up to 2 years after treatment (Fisher & Gilliam, 2012). Recent evidence suggests that TFCO benefits youth with severe antisocial behaviors and may have no significant effects on adolescents with lower risk levels (Sinclair et al., 2016).

COUPLES- AND FAMILY-BASED PROGRAMS FOR ADULT OFFENDERS

Couple and family relationships are one of the four moderate factors known to predict the likelihood of adult criminal conduct (Andrews & Bonta, 2015). When couple and family relationships are high in mutual support, togetherness, and interdependency, they can have a prosocial effect on adult offenders (see Chapter 3). Efforts have been made to translate this empirical knowledge into couple- and family-based interventions for adult correctional populations. These interventions are adaptations of existing evidence-based treatment: PREP Inside and Out, FFT for adult offenders (Datchi & Sexton, 2013), CLFCMEP, SFP, and CRAFT. These programs have been evaluated in pilot studies that have produced promising results. The preliminary findings support the clinical utility of couple and family services to address the relationship-based criminogenic needs of justice-involved adults.

Relationship Education for Couples With a History of Incarceration

PREP Inside Out and CLFCMEP are relationship education and skills training programs designed to promote stable couple relationships (Einhorn et al., 2008; Kazura, 2018; Shamblen et al., 2013). PREP Inside Out focuses on the risk factors that are linked to couple distress, in particular, affect regulation, conflict management, communication, positive connection, and friendship (Einhorn et al., 2008). The program curriculum was tailored to address the unique challenges prisoners experience during incarceration and was tested with a racially diverse sample of male and female inmates in the Oklahoma Department of Corrections. The results showed positive posttreatment effects on relationship satisfaction, commitment, confidence, communication, and friendship for both men and women. Male and female prisoners also experienced a significant decrease in feelings of loneliness and negative interactions with their partners. These findings were partially reproduced in an exploratory study of PREP in the New Hampshire Department of Corrections (Kazura, 2018). At the end of the program, there were significant increases in positive interactions from the perspective of both partners; however, only male inmates reported significant reductions in negative exchanges after treatment, and relationship satisfaction did not change over time.

CLFCMEP is a modified version of Creating Lasting Family Connections, an evidence-based family-focused program originally designed to reduce adolescent substance use (Council on Prevention and Education: Substances, Inc., n.d.). The program curriculum is for couples who have experienced some form of separation because of incarceration, military deployment, or other conditions. It consists of psychoeducation modules that focus on building self-awareness, relationship knowledge, and interpersonal skills for effective communication and conflict resolution (Shamblen et al., 2013). An outcome evaluation of CLFCMEP with married couples showed that the program was effective in improving relationship skills from baseline to follow-up. Both partners (i.e., wives and their incarcerated husbands) in the CLFCMEP group reported higher levels of interpersonal effectiveness compared with the control group (Shamblen et al., 2013). Changes in relationship commitment were observed at the beginning of the intervention; however, they did not last over time.

Family Intervention Programs

Family-focused interventions for adult offenders include parent education, family skills training, and family therapy. SFP is an evidence-based parenting course for caregivers and children that aims to promote family resilience by improving family relationships, parenting skills, and youth's social and life skills (see https://strengtheningfamiliesprogram.org/about/detailed-info/). It was piloted with children of incarcerated parents and their caregivers, and the results indicated that it produced positive changes that lasted up to 4 months after the program ended (A. L. Miller et al., 2013): Caregivers reported lower levels of family conflict, increases in positive parenting, and improved family organization and cohesion.

CRAFT is a skills training program that emphasizes the role of families in the treatment of addiction (Scruggs et al., 2014). It is based on the *community reinforcement approach*, which involves the use of operant conditioning and motivational strategies to change individual behaviors. In CRAFT, families act as a leverage to engage substance-using individuals in treatment and to reduce alcohol- and drug-related problems. Family members or concerned significant others learn positive communication and reinforcement strategies to improve family interactions, remove rewards for substance use, and increase family-based reinforcement for sobriety. CRAFT was tested with serious drug-using offenders in a jail-based facility (J. M. Miller et al., 2016). In addition to family skills training, significant others participated in family counseling with the inmates to assist with the transition from detention to the community. The goal was to enable family members to play a key role in the maintenance of a drug-free lifestyle after incarceration. The evaluation of CRAFT showed that the program had positive effects on offenders' post-release behaviors (J. M. Miller et al., 2016): The CRAFT participants were significantly more likely to pay child support than the comparison group (57% vs. 0%, respectively); they also had 86% lower odds of committing a new crime in the community.

FFT is the only evidence-based family therapy model that has been adapted to serve adult offenders (Datchi & Sexton, 2013). FFT was tailored to target the family processes that are linked to adult criminal conduct: marital discord, family conflict, communication, and problem solving. The adapted FFT model follows the same core principles as the original program; only the treatment target and interventions were altered to address specific risk and protective factors in adult family relationships (Datchi, 2019). The effectiveness of FFT with adult populations was evaluated, and the results showed that offenders reported a significantly reduced odds of recidivating and improved psychological and relational functioning compared with treatment as usual (Datchi & Sexton, 2013). The results also suggested that FFT enhanced family cohesion and organization and decreased family conflict from baseline to termination.

PRACTICE IMPLICATIONS

This chapter has highlighted the extensive contribution of couples and family psychology to research and treatment relevant to violence prevention. Juvenile delinquency has been the primary focus of family intervention science in criminal justice settings. Adult criminal conduct has received less attention, although preliminary evidence suggests that couples and family-based programs help strengthen family relationships and reduce the likelihood of recidivism. The adaptation of empirically supported models such as FFT for adult offenders represents an opportunity to promote new developments in clinical practice with diverse justice populations. It is also an opportunity to improve the family lives of adults under correctional supervision, to support relationship stability, and to promote family resilience. More efforts clearly are needed to describe and evaluate the implementation of well-established couple and family therapy programs with adult offenders.

Family therapy integration represents a method of adapting empirically supported family intervention programs to the unique circumstances of criminal justice populations. Many of these programs (e.g., FFT, MDFT) are theoretically integrative models with specific clinical protocols that are more or less prescriptive in regard to treatment phases, goals, and session activities. They can be tailored by incorporating concepts and interventions that are most relevant to the criminogenic needs of adult offenders. This is referred to as "assimilative integration" (Pitta & Datchi, 2019). Among the frameworks that guide family therapy integration, metatheorical models offer the least restrictive template for treatment (Lebow, 2014): They allow clinicians to select the most effective practices based on their conceptualization of the problem and the best available evidence. Integrative systemic therapy is an example of metatheoretical integration that emphasizes common factors and provides a blueprint for case formulation, treatment planning, and evaluation (Jérémie-Brink & Chambers, 2019). A metatheory of family therapy develops from the specification of metalevel processes of therapeutic change (Lebow, 2014; Sexton et al., 2004). It has the potential to increase treatment flexibility and responsiveness to clients' circumstances. This is all the more important given that many clinicians perceive that empirically supported and manualized programs restrict the exercise of professional judgment (Datchi & Sexton, 2016). A metatheory of clinical practice with justice-involved families has yet to be defined on the basis of current empirical knowledge about effective family therapy models, family dynamics, family resilience, and criminal conduct. Whether such a metatheory may be easier to adopt and implement in criminal justice settings, and whether it may facilitate the dissemination of empirical knowledge and effective interventions into community settings, remains to be seen.

The next chapter concludes the discussion of best clinical practices for justice-involved couples and families. It describes how clinicians apply their knowledge of effective couples- and family-based programs to formulate treatment goals and choose interventions that are client centered. The fictitious case of Sara, Sam, Gabriel, and Julia will serve to illustrate the therapeutic process: how to set goals collaboratively, how to select in-session activities relevant to the presenting issues, and how to monitor progress. Chapter 6 also discusses the role of interprofessional partnerships with other service providers to enhance the effects of family-based interventions.

6 FROM SCIENCE TO PRACTICE

Competency-Based Treatment Planning and Delivery

The preceding chapters have examined the theoretical and scientific literature on delinquency and crime, summarized current knowledge about the predictors of antisocial behaviors, described a relational approach to the assessment and conceptualization of delinquency and criminal conduct, and reported on the effectiveness of systemic intervention programs for justice-involved couples and families. This chapter demonstrates how to integrate and apply the information contained in the previous chapters to the treatment of the fictitious family—Sam, Sara, Gabriel, and Julia—using a competency framework (see the Introduction to this book); specifically, it shows how clinicians use the findings from the family's assessment and case conceptualization to formulate a treatment plan and select interventions that are relevant to the family's presenting concerns, on the basis of the best available science as well as the family members' needs and preferences (Stanton & Welsh, 2011). This concluding chapter discusses treatment monitoring and interprofessional collaboration and calls for increasing the family focus of correctional programming.

---

https://doi.org/10.1037/0000285-007
Best Clinical Practices for Treating Families in Juvenile and Criminal Justice Systems, by C. C. Datchi

SAM, SARA, GABRIEL, AND JULIA: SUMMARY OF FINDINGS

Sara, Gabriel, and Julia entered treatment after Gabriel was arrested for underage drinking and public disturbance. His assessment by the court intake officer showed that Gabriel presented a low to moderate level of risk for recidivism. It also highlighted several key risk factors: low academic performance, alcohol use, antisocial peer influence, and lack of involvement with prosocial institutions in the community. The therapist, Dr. Merlin, conducted a systemic assessment that revealed additional areas of vulnerability: family economic insecurity, parent–child conflict, marital discord, skill deficits in communication and problem solving, low levels of affective involvement, ineffective discipline or behavior control, inconsistent parental supervision, parental stress, and parental substance use. Gabriel's difficulties with emotion regulation were also a concern. Dr. Merlin also identified several strengths of the family, including their social network—in particular, their neighbors, church, and close relatives—which represented a source of prosocial influence and support with adolescent monitoring.

Sam's incarceration resulted in family disruption, ambiguous loss, greater economic instability, and increased parenting stress. The family relationships became more distant and negative as Sara, Gabriel, and Julia struggled with the aftermaths of Sam's involvement with the criminal justice system, including shame and stigma. Their problematic interactions (e.g., blaming, hostility) interfered with their efforts to manage the problems of everyday life and limited Sara's ability to supervise Gabriel and Julia and support their healthy development. Despite these challenges, the family members were loyal to one another and protective of each other. They valued their relationships and worried about their safety and autonomy because of their involvement in the criminal justice system.

TREATMENT PLANNING

Treatment planning is a collaborative process that begins with a discussion of the assessment results and follows with the selection of therapeutic goals and interventions. Collaborative goal setting involves each member of the family and contributes to the strength of the therapeutic alliance (see Chapter 4). Sara, Gabriel, and Julia agreed they would work together to avoid further entanglement with the justice system, protect family unity and autonomy, and prepare for Sam's return home. In their conversations with Dr. Merlin they acknowledged the individual, relational, and environmental factors that undermined their efforts to manage the impact of parental incarceration and keep the family intact. They developed a shared understanding of their difficulties that informed the selection of therapeutic goals and interventions.

Setting Treatment Goals

Dr. Merlin, Sara, Gabriel, and Julia discussed how family therapy would increase the family's capacity to provide protection against multiple risks: antisocial peer influence, family conflict, poor monitoring, ineffective behavior control, and skill deficits in communication and problem solving. They agreed on the following specific treatment goals:

- Promote positivity and emotional bonding by improving the family's communication, problem-solving, and conflict resolution skills and by creating family routines and rituals.
- Increase the family's capacity to support Gabriel and Julia's performance at school by fostering better communication within the family and between the family and the school.
- Enhance the family's ability to reorganize, clarify roles and expectations, and redistribute responsibilities during times of transition (e.g., paternal incarceration and reentry).
- Bolster the family's capacity to utilize the resources of their immediate environment (e.g., relationships with neighbors, church, and close relatives) to improve adult monitoring.

The treatment goals were selected with the purpose of strengthening resilience processes within the family that would act as a buffer against stress and adversity and that would reduce the risks linked to Gabriel's justice involvement. Family resilience called for new interaction patterns that would foster a sense of cohesion and facilitate emotion regulation and the exchange of support and affection; clear family roles, boundaries, and rules; and effective problem-solving and decision-making processes. The treatment goals also required the activation of primary common factors in couples and family therapy (Sprenkle et al., 2009): to engage each family member in the therapeutic process, cocreate a relational understanding of the family's difficulties, and change the family dynamics that contributed to maintain the presenting problems.

Considering the effects of parental incarceration on adolescent behaviors (see Chapter 3), Dr. Merlin, Sara, Gabriel, and Julia discussed the possibility of Sam's participation in treatment to prepare for family reunification.

Dr. Merlin presented information about the challenges of reentry: restoring close bonds with loved ones, resuming previous family roles, easing back into family routines, and managing social disapprobation. Dr. Merlin, Sara, Gabriel, and Julia agreed it would be important to determine how the family would maintain communication with Sam and manage the emotional toll of separation during incarceration.

Selecting Interventions

Given the goals of the family, Dr. Merlin used her knowledge of couples and family psychology science to determine which interventions best matched the clinical needs of Sara, Gabriel, and Julia. First, she considered evidence-based models that were appropriate to Gabriel's behavioral concerns (e.g., delinquency including underage alcohol use) and level of risk for recidivism (i.e., low to moderate). Treatment Foster Care Oregon (TFCO) and multisystemic therapy (MST) are programs designed for chronic and severe juvenile offenders that require intensive and multimodal interventions. The focus of multidimensional family therapy is moderate to severe adolescent substance use and related antisocial behaviors. Functional family therapy (FFT) and brief strategic family therapy have been successfully implemented with low- to high-risk youth to reduce delinquency and substance use (see Chapter 5 for a detailed discussion of these systemic intervention programs). Both FFT and MST were services available at Dr. Merlin's agency. Taking into account Gabriel's behaviors and risk level, Dr. Merlin determined that FFT offered the best fit for the needs and goals of the family.

FFT provides a systematic method of addressing the multilevel factors that predict delinquency and substance use in adolescence. It also provides a structured and coherent framework for achieving the family's treatment goals, for fostering family engagement and motivation, for activating primary common factors (e.g., the therapeutic alliance, new interaction patterns), and for promoting family resilience (Sexton, 2011). Each treatment phase targets specific resilience processes. Phase-specific interventions are designed to produce engagement and motivation and create a shared perception of the problem that supports cohesion and we-ness. Engagement and motivation are the proximal outcomes of the therapist's activities over the course of treatment: using humor, listening tirelessly to understand the family, examining how each individual is part of the solution, and adopting a strengths-based approach to the problem (Sexton, 2011; also see Chapter 4, this volume, for a discussion of engagement in couples and family therapy). These activities show the family that therapy can be useful and foster the creation of therapeutic conditions that reduce negativity and blaming and support emotion regulation and safety. FFT interventions also focus on building skills (e.g., communication, negotiation) that strengthen the family's control system (e.g., ability to monitor and regulate adolescent behaviors). Table 6.1 contains descriptions of the family's treatment goals and corresponding phase-specific objectives and interventions in FFT.

MONITORING TREATMENT PROGRESS AND OUTCOMES

Monitoring treatment progress and outcomes is a critical aspect of evidence-based practice and treatment effectiveness (Sexton & Fisher, 2016; Sexton et al., 2012; Stanton & Welsh, 2011): It involves collecting case-specific data from couples and families to determine the effects of clinical interventions in real time, session by session. The information is used right away to determine how couples and families are responding to treatment and make data-driven and client-centered decisions about the fit of therapeutic goals and interventions. In sum, process and outcome monitoring enhances treatment planning and adaptation. It can also support treatment adherence when clinicians use systematic procedures and psychometrically sound measures that assess client functioning and relevant dimensions of well-established intervention programs (Sexton, 2016; Sexton & Fisher, 2016).

Measurement feedback systems (MFSs) are a recent development in the field of couples and family therapy (Bickman et al., 2012; Pinsof et al., 2012; Sexton & Fisher, 2016). MFSs use new electronic and communication technologies (e.g., cell phones, computers, mobile apps) to facilitate treatment monitoring and promote evidence-based and client-centered clinical decisions. They consist of reliable and valid assessment instruments administered to clients online, before, after, and between sessions. MFSs transform client data instantaneously and produce a feedback report with visual aids that describe progress in individual and relational domains. For example, the FFT Clinical Measurement System is a technology-based MFS designed to track families' response to FFT services and increase therapist's model fidelity, thus improving treatment outcomes (Sexton, 2016; Sexton & Fisher, 2016). It is composed of brief rating scales of individual functioning (e.g., the Patient Health Questionnaire–9; Kroenke et al., 2001), family functioning and stability (e.g., the Alabama Parenting Questionnaire; Frick, 1991), problem severity, therapeutic alliance, and treatment progress and impact. These client and treatment factors are measured from the perspective of youth, caregivers, and therapists (Sexton, n.d.).

TABLE 6.1. Treatment Goals, Phase-Specific Objectives, and Interventions

Treatment phase	Phase-specific objectives	Interventions	Treatment goals
1. Engagement and motivation	Increase focus on family dynamics Cocreate a relational definition of the problem Reduce blaming and negativity Build a balanced therapeutic and within-family alliance	Relational reframing Highlight positive intentions and family strengths Acknowledge the perspectives of family members with empathy	Higher level of positivity, emotional bonding, and family cohesion
2. Behavior change	Build behavioral skills	Teach effective communication and problem-solving skills Practice new skills and behaviors to manage conflict, improve parental supervision, clarify roles and expectations, and negotiate and agree on rules	Increased parental monitoring and family support for improved adolescent functioning, including school performance and peer influence Greater family capacity to reorganize and adapt to transitions
3. Generalization	Generalize new skills and behaviors to various situations and contexts Include community resources into treatment (e.g., referral to mental health services based on individual needs)	Prepare for Sam's reentry and develop a plan for managing issues relevant to family reunification Use new behavioral competencies to improve communication with school and secure external support	Effective use of community resources (e.g., neighbors, extended family, community-based youth programs, assistance programs for low-income families) to increase adult supervision and support success at school and in the community

In Chapter 4, Dr. Merlin selected standardized instruments to gather information about family and individual risk factors (e.g., problem solving, communication, family organization and structure, youth internalizing and externalizing behaviors and peer relationships). The results provided baseline data that would be used to compare family and individual functioning at the beginning and end of treatment. To assess the therapeutic alliance and the family's progress session by session, Dr. Merlin asked Sara, Gabriel, and Julia to complete two questionnaires: The Symptoms and Functioning Severity Scale (Bickman et al., 2010), which can be administered every 2 weeks to measure change in the severity of youth's emotional and behavioral problems and the System for Observing Family Therapy Alliances (Friedlander et al., 2006), a self-report instrument that measures the four dimensions of the family therapy alliance across sessions (i.e., engagement, emotional connection, safety, and a shared sense of purpose). In addition, Dr. Merlin invited the family to share their experience of treatment by asking task-focused questions such as "Did we focus on the right topics today?" and "Did my questions and comments make sense to you?" (Maeschalck & Barfknecht, 2017). Dr. Merlin encouraged the family's honesty, demonstrated openness to feedback, and used the information they provided to make treatment adaptations that were responsive to their needs and preferences.

COLLABORATING WITH OTHER PROFESSIONALS

At the beginning of treatment, Dr. Merlin informed the family that she would communicate with Gabriel's probation officer about the family's attendance at therapy. She also explained how she would report on the family's progress at the end of therapy. Relapse is a normal occurrence during treatment: She informed them that if Gabriel experienced behavioral difficulties that resulted in further justice intervention, she may need to contact the probation officer to discuss the best course of action and prevent treatment disruption.

Dr. Merlin obtained Sara's consent to exchange information with Gabriel's school. Her goals were to understand Gabriel's behaviors from the perspective of his teachers and to work with the school to increase Gabriel's school engagement and enhance his academic performance. In particular, Dr. Merlin and the school agreed to review Gabriel's individualized educational program, remove barriers to Sara's involvement in the individualized educational program meetings, and use community resources (e.g., after-school mentoring and team sports) to create contextual protective factors in Gabriel's everyday life.

Dr. Merlin also received Sara's permission to contact Sam's case manager at the jail and discuss the possibility of his participation in treatment. The jail had a telehealth consultation room equipped with a computer and telemedicine software, whereby inmates received psychiatric and other specialty care. The room offered some privacy: The jail staff could not hear the session; however, they could use the surveillance camera to monitor inmates' movement. Dr. Merlin and Sam's case manager assessed the family's level of comfort with technology, discussed the limits of confidentiality in telebehavioral health and correctional settings, and developed a schedule for when Sam would join the therapy sessions remotely. Dr. Merlin, the case manager, Sara, and Sam understood that external factors (e.g., emergency appointments, a low number of security staff available to supervise the telehealth appointments) may disrupt Sam's participation schedule. For this reason, as long as Sam remained in detention, they chose to focus on goals and activities that would support family reunification in the last phase of treatment: Sam, Sara, Gabriel, and Julia would work together to develop a family reentry plan with clear family roles, expectations, and rituals; they would also practice effective communication and problem solving in preparation for future challenges. Dr. Merlin would collaborate with Sam's case manager on the family's aftercare plan and make recommendations for additional services, such as couples therapy.

TREATMENT CHALLENGES AND SUCCESSES

Treatment engagement, retention, and completion are common challenges to court-mandated clients like Sara, Gabriel, and Julia. Legal coercion is a mechanism of extrinsic motivation that does not automatically result in client attendance and active participation in therapeutic activities. Research suggests that the quality of the therapeutic alliance moderates clients' experience of treatment as involuntary; in particular, characteristics such as a caring attitude, fairness, trust, and respect can offset the negative effects of legal coercion and promote engagement and motivation (Hachtel et al., 2019).

Dr. Merlin used the Symptoms and Functioning Severity Scale to monitor the strength of the therapeutic alliance with Sara, Gabriel, and Julia. Every week, she reviewed individual items on the questionnaire to identify clinical areas that needed attention. By the third week of treatment, she noted low scores on Gabriel's assessment of the therapeutic alliance: He reported that Dr. Merlin understood him a little; he also endorsed the statement that "some family members don't agree with others about the goals of therapy." When Sara rescheduled the fourth therapy session, Dr. Merlin called the family to explore and address the risks for retention. During the phone conversation, she used reframing to discuss the family's difficulties in the past week and emphasize the relational nature of their concerns, and to thus increase their level of engagement and motivation. She talked with each of them separately and together for about 45 minutes. With Gabriel, she focused on their therapeutic bond: She asked him interested questions about his gaming hobby and worked hard to communicate understanding. In the conversation, Dr. Merlin also learned that Sara's car was at the repair shop; she informed Sara that she would arrange free transportation for the family for the following 2 weeks.

Transportation was not the only barrier to the family's treatment. Session scheduling and phone contact also proved challenging; they are common hurdles in clinical practice with justice-involved populations. Dr. Merlin met with the family on the weekends or late in the evening to accommodate Sara's work hours. Before each scheduled session, she called the family to confirm their appointment and address difficulties that may prevent attendance. Midway through treatment, Sara's phone number was disconnected, and Dr. Merlin worked with Gabriel's probation officer to reestablish contact with the family, secure resources to support therapist–client communication, and obtain permission to contact Sara's next-door neighbor if needed.

Sara, Gabriel, and Julia completed treatment in 5 months and participated in a total of 15 sessions. Sam joined the family in the last phase of therapy to discuss and plan for family reunification. Sara participated in two conjoint sessions with Sam only. As they discussed expectations about coparenting, family roles, and family rules, Sara also practiced, with Dr. Merlin's support and encouragement, effective communication and problem-solving skills in the couple relationship. At termination, Sam and Sara were referred to a community-based organization that offered reentry services and assistance with housing, employment, and family reunification. Gabriel had returned to school and was participating in a mentoring program in which he was paired with a college student. The family also received a 1-year membership to the local YMCA, where Julia and Gabriel spent time after school. Treatment was successful in strengthening the family's resilience processes (i.e., communication, problem solving, positivity, and emotional bonding) and reducing family and contextual risk factors such as family conflict and antisocial peer influence. It was also successful in connecting the family with prosocial community resources.

FINAL THOUGHTS

Families in the juvenile and criminal justice system experience complex psychological and social problems: substance use disorders, trauma, mental illness, disabilities, low educational attainment, poverty, and unemployment.

They also present a multitude of individual, relational, and contextual risk factors that increase the odds of repeated contact with law enforcement and corrections. This book has provided an overview of current empirical knowledge about the effects of couple and family dynamics on the trajectory of delinquency and crime. It has described a family systems and competency-based approach to the treatment of juvenile and adult offenders that integrates up-to-date evidence about the common and specific factors of effective interventions with correctional populations. The relational contexts of antisocial behaviors constitute a site of intervention to activate resilience processes in individuals' extended family system, promote offenders' involvement in prosocial family roles and activities, and increase families' capacity to function as a buffer against risks.

This book has presented arguments in support of increased couples and family programming in correctional settings (e.g., probation, parole, jail, prison). Despite growing evidence, there is still limited access to effective couple and family interventions for offender populations. This includes empirically supported treatment models like MST, FFT, and TFCO. On average, across the United States, these programs are scarce. A majority of states (25 out of 35) have only one or two FFT, MST, or TFCO sites (Welsh & Greenwood, 2015). A few states are leading the way in the large-scale use of effective family therapy programs with a median number of 10.6 FFT, MST, and TFCO teams: New Mexico, Louisiana, Maine, Connecticut, and Hawaii. Their relative success provides insight into the factors that promote the dissemination of family-focused evidence-based practices in juvenile justice settings: These states identified and brought together key stakeholders and experts to champion the adoption of evidence-based programs and guide the process of implementing and testing pilot programs; they also allocated special funds to support the local expansion of select evidence-based practices (Welsh & Greenwood, 2015).

Positive family involvement is an important concern and objective in juvenile justice in particular (Burke et al., 2014). Evidence-based couples and family therapy models represent one strategy for engaging families in correctional services. Future efforts are needed to operationalize, implement, and evaluate family-focused models of juvenile and criminal justice that recognize family relationships as a powerful support system, emphasize respect and collaborative decision making, and describe formal mechanisms for optimal family involvement.

References

Aaron, L., & Dallaire, D. H. (2010). Parental incarceration and multiple risk experiences: Effects on family dynamics and children's delinquency. *Journal of Youth and Adolescence, 39*(12), 1471–1484. https://doi.org/10.1007/s10964-009-9458-0

Abeling-Judge, D. (2016). Different social influences and desistance from crime. *Criminal Justice and Behavior, 43*(9), 1225–1241. https://doi.org/10.1177/0093854816652639

Alarid, L. F., & Rangel, L. M., Jr. (2018). Completion and recidivism rates of high-risk youth on probation: Do home visits make a difference? *The Prison Journal, 98*(2), 143–162. https://doi.org/10.1177/0032885517753152

Alexander, J. F., Waldron, H. B., Robbins, M. S., & Neeb, A. A. (2013). *Functional family therapy for adolescent behavior problems.* American Psychological Association. https://doi.org/10.1037/14139-000

Alper, M., Durose, M. R., & Markman, J. (2018). *2018 update on prisoner recidivism: A 9-year follow-up period (2005–2014)*. U.S. Department of Justice. https://www.bjs.gov/content/pub/pdf/18upr9yfup0514.pdf

Amani, B., Milburn, N. G., Lopez, S., Young-Brinn, A., Castro, L., Lee, A., & Bath, E. (2018). Families and the juvenile justice system: Considerations for family-based interventions. *Family & Community Health, 41*(1), 55–63. https://doi.org/10.1097/FCH.0000000000000172

Amatya, P. L., & Barzman, D. H. (2012). The missing link between juvenile delinquency and pediatric posttraumatic stress disorder: An attachment theory lens. *ISRN Pediatrics, 2012*, 134541. https://doi.org/10.5402/2012/134541

American Psychiatric Association. (2017). *Mental health disparities: Diverse populations*. https://www.psychiatry.org/psychiatrists/cultural-competency/education/mental-health-facts

Andrews, D. A., & Bonta, J. (2015). *The psychology of criminal conduct* (5th ed.). Anderson Publishing.

The Annie E. Casey Foundation. (2016, April 19). *Children of incarcerated parents, a shared sentence: The devastating toll of parental incarceration on kids, families and communities*. https://www.aecf.org/resources/a-shared-sentence

APA Presidential Task Force on Evidence-Based Practice. (2006). Evidence-based practice in psychology. *American Psychologist, 61*(4), 271–285. https://doi.org/10.1037/0003-066X.61.4.271

Apel, R. (2016). The effects of jail and prison confinement on cohabitation and marriage. *The Annals of the American Academy of Political and Social Science, 665*(1), 103–126. https://doi.org/10.1177/0002716216629360

Arditti, J. A. (2016). A family stress-proximal process model for understanding the effects of parental incarceration on children and their families. *Couple & Family Psychology, 5*(2), 65–88. https://doi.org/10.1037/cfp0000058

Åström, T., Bergström, M., Håkansson, K., Jonsson, A. K., Munthe, C., Wirtberg, I., Wiss, J., & Sundell, K. (2020). Treatment Foster Care Oregon for delinquent adolescents: A systematic review and meta-analysis. *Research on Social Work Practice, 30*(4), 355–367. https://doi.org/10.1177/1049731519890394

Ayón, C., Williams, L. R., Marsiglia, F. F., Ayers, S., & Kiehne, E. (2015). A latent profile analysis of Latino parenting: The infusion of cultural values on family conflict. *Families in Society, 96*(3), 203–210. https://doi.org/10.1606/1044-3894.2015.96.25

Azeredo, A., Moreira, D., Figueiredo, P., & Barbosa, F. (2019). Delinquent behavior: Systematic review of genetic and environmental risk factors. *Clinical Child and Family Psychology Review, 22*(4), 502–526. https://doi.org/10.1007/s10567-019-00298-w

Baggio, S., Heller, P., Barnert, E. S., Tran, N. T., Getaz, L., & Wolff, H. (2019). Substance use initiation among justice-involved youths: Evidence from the Pathways to Desistance Study. *Journal of Child & Adolescent Substance Abuse, 28*(2), 73–82. https://doi.org/10.1080/1067828X.2019.1578711

Baglivio, M. T., Epps, N., Swartz, K., Huq, M. S., Sheer, A., & Hardt, N. S. (2014). The prevalence of adverse childhood experiences in the lives of juvenile offenders. *Journal of Juvenile Justice, 3*(2). https://www.prisonpolicy.org/scans/Prevalence_of_ACE.pdf

Baglivio, M. T., Jackowski, K., Greenwald, M. A., & Wolff, K. T. (2014). Comparison of multisystemic therapy and functional family therapy effectiveness: A multiyear statewide propensity score matching analysis of juvenile offenders. *Criminal Justice and Behavior, 41*(9), 1033–1056. https://doi.org/10.1177/0093854814543272

Baldwin, S. A., Christian, S., Berkeljon, A., & Shadish, W. R. (2012). The effects of family therapies for adolescent delinquency and substance abuse: A meta-analysis. *Journal of Marital and Family Therapy, 38*(1), 281–304. https://doi.org/10.1111/j.1752-0606.2011.00248.x

Baranyi, G., Cassidy, M., Fazel, S., Priebe, S., & Mundt, A. P. (2018). Prevalence of posttraumatic stress disorder in prisoners. *Epidemiologic Reviews, 40*(1), 134–145. https://doi.org/10.1093/epirev/mxx015

Barnao, M. T., Ward, T., & Robertson, P. D. (2015). The Good Lives Model: A new paradigm for forensic mental health. *Psychiatry, Psychology and Law*, *23*(2), 1–14. https://doi.org/10.1080/13218719.2015.1054923

Barnert, E. S., Perry, R., Azzi, V. F., Shetgiri, R., Ryan, G., Dudovitz, R., Zima, B., & Chung, P. J. (2015). Incarcerated youths' perspectives on protective factors and risk factors for juvenile offending: A qualitative analysis. *American Journal of Public Health*, *105*(7), 1365–1371. https://doi.org/10.2105/AJPH.2014.302228

Beach, S. R. H., Wamboldt, M. Z., Kaslow, N. J., Heyman, R., & Reiss, D. (2006). Relational processes and mental health: A bench to bedside dialogue to guide the *DSM–V*. In S. R. H. Beach, M. Wamboldt, N. Kaslow, R. E. Heyman, M. First, L. G. Underwood, & D. Reiss (Eds.), *Relational processes and DSM–V: Neuroscience, assessment, prevention, and treatment* (pp. 1–20). American Psychiatric Press.

Beardslee, J., Miltimore, S., Fine, A., Frick, P. J., Steinberg, L., & Cauffman, E. (2019). Under the radar or under arrest: How is adolescent boys' first contact with the juvenile justice system related to future offending and arrests? *Law and Human Behavior*, *43*(4), 342–357. https://doi.org/10.1037/lhb0000340

Beavers, R., & Hampson, R. B. (2000). The Beavers systems model of family functioning. *Journal of Family Therapy*, *22*(2), 128–143. https://doi.org/10.1111/1467-6427.00143

Beavers, W. R., & Hampson, R. B. (2003). Measuring family competence: The Beavers systems model. In F. Walsh (Ed.), *Normal family processes: Growing diversity and complexity* (3rd ed., pp. 549–580). Guilford Press. https://doi.org/10.4324/9780203428436_chapter_20

Becker, K. D., Kiser, L. J., Herr, S. R., Stapleton, L. M., Barksdale, C. L., & Buckingham, S. (2014). Changes in treatment engagement of youths and families with complex needs. *Children and Youth Services Review*, *46*, 276–284. https://doi.org/10.1016/j.childyouth.2014.09.005

Belenko, S., Hiller, M., & Hamilton, L. (2013). Treating substance use disorders in the criminal justice system. *Current Psychiatry Reports*, *15*(11), Article 414. https://doi.org/10.1007/s11920-013-0414-z

Bergström, M., & Höjman, L. (2016). Is multidimensional treatment foster care (MTFC) more effective than treatment as usual in a three-year follow-up? Results from MTFC in a Swedish setting. *European Journal of Social Work*, *19*(2), 219–235. https://doi.org/10.1080/13691457.2015.1030361

Berman, G. (2009). Problem solving justice and the moment of truth. In P. Higgins & M. B. Mackinem (Eds.), *Problem solving courts: Justice for the twenty first century?* (pp. 1–11). ABC Clio.

Bersani, B. E., & Doherty, E. E. (2013). When the ties that bind unwind: Examining the enduring and situational processes of change behind the marriage effect. *Criminology*, *51*(2), 399–433. https://doi.org/10.1111/1745-9125.12008

Bickman, L., Athay, M. M., Riemer, M., Lambert, E. W., Kelley, S. D., Breda, C., Tempesti, T., Dew-Reeves, S. E., Brannan, A. M., & Vides de Andrade, A. R. (Eds.). (2010). *Manual of the Peabody Treatment Progress Battery* (2nd ed.)

[Electronic version]. Center for Evaluation and Program Improvement, Vanderbilt University. https://peabody.vanderbilt.edu/docs/pdf/cepi/ptpb_2nd_ed/PTPB_2010_Entire_Manual_UPDATE_31212.pdf

Bickman, L., Kelley, S. D., & Athay, M. (2012). The technology of measurement feedback systems. *Couple & Family Psychology, 1*(4), 274–284. https://doi.org/10.1037/a0031022

Blanchette, K., & Brown, S. L. (2019). Female offenders. In R. Morgan (Ed.), *The Sage encyclopedia of criminal psychology* (Vol. 1, pp. 490–495). Sage. https://doi.org/10.4135/9781483392240.n163

Blankestein, A., van der Rijken, R., Eeren, H. V., Lange, A., Scholte, R., Moonen, X., De Vuyst, K., Leunissen, J., & Didden, R. (2019). Evaluating the effects of multisystemic therapy for adolescents with intellectual disabilities and antisocial or delinquent behaviour and their parents. *Journal of Applied Research in Intellectual Disabilities, 32*(3), 575–590. https://doi.org/10.1111/jar.12551

Blueprints for Healthy Youth Development. (n.d.). *Experimentally proven programs*. https://www.blueprintsprograms.org/

Boldt, R. C. (2009). A circumspect look at problem solving courts. In P. Higgins & M. B. Mackinem (Eds.), *Problem solving courts: Justice for the twenty first century?* (pp. 13–31). ABC Clio.

Bonta, J. (2019). Psychology of Criminal Conduct. In R. D. Morgan (Ed.), *The Sage encyclopedia of criminal psychology* (pp. 1145–1149). Sage. https://doi.org/10.4135/9781483392240.n372

Borduin, C. M., & Dopp, A. R. (2015). Economic impact of multisystemic therapy with juvenile sexual offenders. *Journal of Family Psychology, 29*(5), 687–696. https://doi.org/10.1037/fam0000113

Boss, P. (1999). *Ambiguous loss: Learning to live with unresolved grief*. Harvard University Press.

Boss, P. (2016). The context and process of theory development: The story of ambiguous loss. *Journal of Family Theory & Review, 8*(3), 269–286. https://doi.org/10.1111/jftr.12152

Boxer, P., Docherty, M., Ostermann, M., Kubik, J., & Veysey, B. (2017). Effectiveness of Multisystemic Therapy for gang-involved youth offenders: One year follow-up analysis of recidivism outcomes. *Children and Youth Services Review, 73*, 107–112. https://doi.org/10.1016/j.childyouth.2016.12.008

Bray, J. H. (2009). Couple and family assessment. In J. H. Bray & M. Stanton (Eds.), *The Wiley-Blackwell handbook of family psychology* (pp. 151–164). Blackwell. https://doi.org/10.1002/9781444310238.ch10

Bright, C. L., Sacco, P., Kolivoski, K. M., Stapleton, L. M., Jun, H. J., & Morris-Compton, D. (2017). Gender differences in patterns of substance use and delinquency: A latent transition analysis. *Journal of Child & Adolescent Substance Abuse, 26*(2), 162–173. https://doi.org/10.1080/1067828X.2016.1242100

Bronson, J., & Berzofsky, M. (2017, June). *Indicators of mental health problems reported by prisoners and jail inmates, 2011–12*. U.S. Department of Justice,

Office of Justice Programs, Bureau of Justice Statistics. https://bjs.ojp.gov/content/pub/pdf/imhprpji1112.pdf

Bronson, J., & Carson, E. A. (2019, April). *Prisoners in 2017*. U.S. Department of Justice, Office of Justice Programs, Bureau of Justice Statistics. https://www.bjs.gov/content/pub/pdf/p17.pdf

Bronson, J., Stroop, J., Zimmer, S., & Berzofsky, M. (2017). *Drug use, dependence, and abuse among state prisoners and jail inmates, 2007–2009*. U.S. Department of Justice, Office of Justice Programs, Bureau of Justice Statistics. https://www.bjs.gov/content/pub/pdf/dudaspji0709.pdf

Brown, S. L., Blanchette, K., & Thapa, S. (2019). Female offenders: Prevalence and statistics. In R. Morgan (Ed.), *The Sage encyclopedia of criminal psychology* (Vol. 1, pp. 507–509). Sage. https://www.doi.org/10.4135/9781483392240.n167

Brown, S. M., & Shillington, A. M. (2017). Childhood adversity and the risk of substance use and delinquency: The role of protective adult relationships. *Child Abuse & Neglect, 63*, 211–221. https://doi.org/10.1016/j.chiabu.2016.11.006

Burke, J. D., Mulvey, E. P., Schubert, C. A., & Garbin, S. R. (2014). The challenge and opportunity of parental involvement in juvenile justice services. *Children and Youth Services Review, 39*, 39–47. https://doi.org/10.1016/j.childyouth.2014.01.007

Burling, A. (2018). *Race in the criminal justice system*. Essential Library.

Calzada, E. J., Fernandez, Y., & Cortes, D. E. (2010). Incorporating the cultural value of *respeto* into a framework of Latino parenting. *Cultural Diversity & Ethnic Minority Psychology, 16*(1), 77–86. https://doi.org/10.1037/a0016071

Carr, A. (2016). The evolution of systems theory. In T. L. Sexton & J. Lebow (Eds.), *Handbook of family therapy* (pp. 13–29). Routledge.

Carr, A. (2019). Couple therapy, family therapy and systemic interventions for adult-focused problems: The current evidence base. *Journal of Family Therapy, 41*(4), 492–536. https://doi.org/10.1111/1467-6427.12225

Carr, A., & Stratton, P. (2017). The SCORE family assessment questionnaire: A decade of progress. *Family Process, 56*(2), 285–301. https://doi.org/10.1111/famp.12280

Casas, J. M. (2017). *Handbook of multicultural counseling* (4th ed.). Sage. https://doi.org/10.4135/9781506304458

Cavanagh, C., & Cauffman, E. (2017). The longitudinal association of relationship quality and reoffending among first-time juvenile offenders and their mothers. *Journal of Youth and Adolescence, 46*(7), 1533–1546. https://doi.org/10.1007/s10964-017-0679-3

Celinska, K., Sung, H., Kim, C., & Valdimarsdottir, M. (2019). An outcome evaluation of Functional Family Therapy for court-involved youth. *Journal of Family Therapy, 41*(2), 251–276. https://doi.org/10.1111/1467-6427.12224

Centers for Disease Control and Prevention. (2020, April 3). *Behavioral risk factor surveillance system ACE data*. https://www.cdc.gov/violenceprevention/childabuseandneglect/acestudy/ace-brfss.html

Chamberlain, P. (2003). *Treating chronic juvenile offenders: Advances made through the Oregon Multidimensional Treatment Foster Care Model*. American Psychological Association. https://doi.org/10.1037/10596-000

Chen, P., Voisin, D. R., & Jacobson, K. C. (2016). Community violence exposure and adolescent delinquency: Examining a spectrum of promotive factors. *Youth & Society*, *48*(1), 33–57. https://doi.org/10.1177/0044118X13475827

Chen, W.-Y., Propp, J., deLara, E., & Corvo, K. (2011). Child neglect and its association with subsequent juvenile drug and alcohol offense. *Child & Adolescent Social Work Journal*, *28*(4), 273–290. https://doi.org/10.1007/s10560-011-0232-2

Cho, M., Haight, W., Choi, W. S., Hong, S., & Piescher, K. (2019). A prospective, longitudinal study of risk factors for early onset of delinquency among maltreated youth. *Children and Youth Services Review*, *102*, 222–230. https://doi.org/10.1016/j.childyouth.2019.05.023

Cloud, D., Dougherty, M., May, R. L., II, Parsons, J., Wormeli, P., & Rudman, W. J. (2014). At the intersection of health and justice. *Perspectives in Health Information Management*, *11*(Winter), Article 1c.

Comfort, M. (2016). "A twenty-hour-a-day job": The impact of frequent low-level criminal justice involvement on family life. *The Annals of the American Academy of Political and Social Science*, *665*(1), 63–79. https://doi.org/10.1177/0002716215625038

Comfort, M., McKay, T. E., Landwehr, J. G., Kennedy, E. K., Lindquist, C. H., & Bir, A. (2016). The costs of incarceration for families of prisoners. *International Review of the Red Cross*, *98*(903), 783–798. https://doi.org/10.1017/S1816383117000704

Conrad, S. M., Tolou-Shams, M., Rizzo, C. J., Placella, N., & Brown, L. K. (2014). Gender differences in recidivism rates for juvenile justice youth: The impact of sexual abuse. *Law and Human Behavior*, *38*(4), 305–314. https://doi.org/10.1037/lhb0000062

Couloute, L. (2018, October). *Getting back on course: Educational exclusion and attainment among formerly incarcerated people*. Prison Policy Initiative. https://www.prisonpolicy.org/reports/education.html

Couloute, L., & Kopf, D. (2018, July). *Out of prison & out of work: Unemployment among formerly incarcerated people*. Prison Policy Initiative. https://www.prisonpolicy.org/reports/outofwork.html

Council on Prevention and Education: Substances, Inc. (n.d.). *Creating Lasting Family Connections curriculum series*. https://copes.org/wp-content/uploads/2015/04/CLFC-Series-Brochure.pdf

Curcio, A. L., Mak, A. S., & George, A. M. (2013). Do adolescent delinquency and problem drinking share psychosocial risk factors? A literature review. *Addictive Behaviors*, *38*(4), 2003–2013. https://doi.org/10.1016/j.addbeh.2012.12.004

Dakof, G. A., Henderson, C. E., Rowe, C. L., Boustani, M., Greenbaum, P. E., Wang, W., Hawes, S., Linares, C., & Liddle, H. A. (2015). A randomized clinical trial of family therapy in juvenile drug court. *Journal of Family Psychology, 29*(2), 232–241. https://doi.org/10.1037/fam0000053

Dalton, E. J., Greenman, P. S., Classen, C. C., & Johnson, S. M. (2013). Nurturing connections in the aftermath of childhood trauma: A randomized controlled trial of emotionally focused couple therapy for female survivors of childhood abuse. *Couple & Family Psychology, 2*(3), 209–221. https://doi.org/10.1037/a0032772

Darnell, A. J., & Schuler, M. S. (2015). Quasi-experimental study of functional family therapy effectiveness for juvenile justice aftercare in a racially and ethnically diverse community sample. *Children and Youth Services Review, 50*, 75–82. https://doi.org/10.1016/j.childyouth.2015.01.013

Datchi, C. C. (2017a). Masculinities, fatherhood, and desistance from crime: Moderating and mediating processes involved in men's criminal conduct. *Journal of Men's Studies, 25*(1), 44–69. https://doi.org/10.1177/1060826516641100

Datchi, C. C. (2017b). Women and adult drug treatment courts: Surveillance, social conformity, and the exercise of agency. In C. C. Datchi & J. R. Ancis (Eds.), *Gender, psychology and justice: The mental health of women and girls in the legal system* (pp. 101–126). New York University Press. https://doi.org/10.18574/nyu/9781479819850.003.0005

Datchi, C. C. (2019). Functional family therapy with couples behind bars. In P. J. Pitta & C. C. Datchi (Eds.), *Integrative couple and family therapies: Treatment models for complex clinical issues* (pp. 157–178). American Psychological Association. https://doi.org/10.1037/0000151-008

Datchi, C. C., & Ancis, J. R. (Eds.). (2017). *Gender, psychology, and justice: The mental health of women and girls in the legal system*. New York University Press.

Datchi, C. C., Barretti, L. M., & Thompson, C. M. (2016). Family services in adult detention centers: Systemic principles for prisoner reentry. *Couple & Family Psychology, 5*(2), 89–104. https://doi.org/10.1037/cfp0000057

Datchi, C. C., & Sexton, T. L. (2013). Can family therapy have an effect on adult criminal conduct? Initial evaluation of functional family therapy. *Couple & Family Psychology, 2*(4), 278–293. https://doi.org/10.1037/a0034166

Datchi, C. C., & Sexton, T. L. (2016). Integrating research and practice through intervention science: New developments in family therapy research. In T. L. Sexton & J. Lebow (Eds.), *Handbook of family therapy* (pp. 434–453). Routledge/Taylor & Francis.

DeHart, D., Lynch, S., Belknap, J., Dass-Brailsford, P., & Green, B. (2014). Life history models of female offending: The roles of serious mental illness and trauma in women's pathways to jail. *Psychology of Women Quarterly, 38*(1), 138–151. https://doi.org/10.1177/0361684313494357

Deković, M., Asscher, J. J., Manders, W. A., Prins, P. J. M., & van der Laan, P. (2012). Within-intervention change: Mediators of intervention effects during multisystemic therapy. *Journal of Consulting and Clinical Psychology, 80*(4), 574–587. https://doi.org/10.1037/a0028482

Dierkhising, C. B., Ko, S. J., Woods-Jaeger, B., Briggs, E. C., Lee, R., & Pynoos, R. S. (2013). Trauma histories among justice-involved youth: Findings from the National Child Traumatic Stress Network. *European Journal of Psychotraumatology, 4*. https://doi.org/10.3402/ejpt.v4i0.20274

Doherty, E. E., & Bersani, B. E. (2016). Understanding the mechanisms of desistance at the intersection of race, gender, and neighborhood context. *Journal of Research in Crime and Delinquency, 53*(5), 681–710. https://doi.org/10.1177/0022427816632573

Doherty, E. E., & Ensminger, M. E. (2013). Marriage and offending among a cohort of disadvantaged African Americans. *Journal of Research in Crime and Delinquency, 50*(1), 104–131. https://doi.org/10.1177/0022427811423106

Dolan, K. (2015, March 18). *The poor get prison: The alarming spread of the criminalization of poverty*. Institute for Policy Studies. https://ips-dc.org/the-poor-get-prison-the-alarming-spread-of-the-criminalization-of-poverty/

Dopp, A. R., Borduin, C. M., White, M. H., II, & Kuppens, S. (2017). Family-based treatments for serious juvenile offenders: A multilevel meta-analysis. *Journal of Consulting and Clinical Psychology, 85*(4), 335–354. https://doi.org/10.1037/ccp0000183

Dopp, A. R., Coen, A. S., Smith, A. B., Reno, J., Bernstein, D. H., Kerns, S. E. U., & Altschul, D. (2018). Economic impact of the statewide implementation of an evidence-based treatment: Multisystemic therapy in New Mexico. *Behavior Therapy, 49*(4), 551–566. https://doi.org/10.1016/j.beth.2017.12.003

Duke, B. (2018). A meta-analysis comparing educational attainment prior to incarceration and recidivism rates in relation to correctional education. *Journal of Correctional Education, 69*(1), 44–59.

Durose, M. R., Cooper, A. D., & Snyder, H. N. (2014, April). *Recidivism of prisoners released in 30 states in 2005: Patterns from 2005 to 2010*. U.S. Department of Justice, Office of Justice Programs, Bureau of Justice Statistics. https://www.bjs.gov/content/pub/pdf/rprts05p0510.pdf

Eeren, H. V., Goossens, L. M. A., Scholte, R. H. J., Busschbach, J. J. V., & van der Rijken, R. E. A. (2018). Multisystemic therapy and functional family therapy compared on their effectiveness using the propensity score method. *Journal of Abnormal Child Psychology, 46*(5), 1037–1050. https://doi.org/10.1007/s10802-017-0392-4

Ehrmann, S., Hyland, N., & Puzzanchera, C. (2019, April). *Girls in the juvenile justice system*. U.S. Department of Justice, Office of Justice Programs, Office of Juvenile Justice and Delinquency Prevention. https://ojjdp.ojp.gov/sites/g/files/xyckuh176/files/pubs/251486.pdf

Einhorn, L., Williams, T., Stanley, S., Wunderlin, N., Markman, H., & Eason, J. (2008). PREP inside and out: Marriage education for inmates. *Family Process, 47*(3), 341–356. https://doi.org/10.1111/j.1545-5300.2008.00257.x

Enns, P. K., Yi, Y., Comfort, M., Goldman, A. W., Lee, H., Muller, C., Wakefield, S., Wang, E. A., & Wildeman, C. (2019). What percentage of Americans have ever had a family member incarcerated? Evidence from the Family History of

Incarceration Survey (FamHIS). *Socius, 5*, 1–45. https://doi.org/10.1177/2378023119829332

Epstein, N. B., Baldwin, L. M., & Bishop, D. S. (1983). The McMaster Family Assessment Device. *Journal of Marital and Family Therapy, 9*(2), 171–180. https://doi.org/10.1111/j.1752-0606.1983.tb01497.x

Epstein, N. B., Ryan, C. E., Bishop, D. S., Miller, I. W., & Keitner, G. I. (2003). The McMaster model: A view of healthy family functioning. In F. Walsh (Ed.), *Normal family processes: Growing diversity and complexity* (3rd ed., pp. 581–607). Guilford Press. https://doi.org/10.4324/9780203428436_chapter_21

Evans, S. Z., Simons, L. G., & Simons, R. L. (2016). Factors that influence trajectories of delinquency throughout adolescence. *Journal of Youth and Adolescence, 45*(1), 156–171. https://doi.org/10.1007/s10964-014-0197-5

Ewert, S., & Wildhagen, T. (2011, March 31–April 2). *Educational characteristics of prisoners: Data from ACS* [Paper]. Annual Meeting of the Population Association of America, Washington, DC. https://www.census.gov/content/dam/Census/library/working-papers/2011/demo/ewert-wildhagen-prisoner-education-4-6-11.pdf

Fabio, A., Tu, L.-C., Loeber, R., & Cohen, J. (2011). Neighborhood socioeconomic disadvantage and the shape of the age–crime curve. *American Journal of Public Health, 101*(Suppl. 1), S325–S332. https://doi.org/10.2105/AJPH.2010.300034

Facer-Irwin, E., Blackwood, N. J., Bird, A., Dickson, H., McGlade, D., Alves-Costa, F., & MacManus, D. (2019). PTSD in prison settings: A systematic review and meta-analysis of comorbid mental disorders and problematic behaviours. *PLOS ONE, 14*(9), e0222407. https://doi.org/10.1371/journal.pone.0222407

Fagan, A. A., Van Horn, M. L., Antaramian, S., & Hawkins, J. D. (2011). How do families matter? Age and gender differences in family influences on delinquency and drug use. *Youth Violence and Juvenile Justice, 9*(2), 150–170. https://doi.org/10.1177/1541204010377748

Farrington, D. P. (2019). The development of violence from age 8 to 61. *Aggressive Behavior, 45*(4), 365–376. https://doi.org/10.1002/ab.21831

Farrington, D. P., Ttofi, M., & Piquero, A. R. (2016). Risk, promotive, and protective factors in youth offending: Results from the Cambridge Study in Delinquent Development. *Journal of Criminal Justice, 45*, 63–70. https://doi.org/10.1016/j.jcrimjus.2016.02.014

Farrington, D. P., & Welsh, B. C. (2006). *Saving children from a life of crime: Early risk factors and effective interventions*. Oxford University Press. https://doi.org/10.1093/acprof:oso/9780195304091.001.0001

Fearn, N. E., Vaughn, M. G., Nelson, E. J., Salas-Wright, C. P., DeLisi, M., & Qian, Z. (2016). Trends and correlates of substance use disorders among probationers and parolees in the United States 2002–2014. *Drug and Alcohol Dependence, 167*, 128–139. https://doi.org/10.1016/j.drugalcdep.2016.08.003

Federal Bureau of Investigation. (2019). *Uniform Crime Report: Crime in the United States, 2018. Arrests*. https://ucr.fbi.gov/crime-in-the-u.s/2018/crime-in-the-u.s.-2018/topic-pages/persons-arrested.pdf

Federal Bureau of Prisons. (2020, July 10). *Offenses* [Table]. https://www.bop.gov/about/statistics/statistics_inmate_offenses.jsp

Federal Interagency Forum on Child and Family Statistics. (2019). *America's children: Key national indicators of well-being, 2019*. U.S. Government Printing Office. https://www.childstats.gov/pdf/ac2019/ac_19.pdf

Ferguson, K. T., & Evans, G. W. (2019). Social ecological theory: Family systems and family psychology in bioecological and bioecocultural perspective. In B. H. Fiese, M. Celano, K. Deater-Deckard, E. N. Jouriles, & M. A. Whisman (Eds.), *APA handbook of contemporary family psychology: Foundations, methods, and contemporary issues across the lifespan* (pp. 143–161). American Psychological Association. https://doi.org/10.1037/0000099-009

Fiese, B. H., Jones, B. L., & Saltzman, J. A. (2019). Systems unify family psychology. In B. H. Fiese, M. Celano, K. Deater-Deckard, E. N. Jouriles, & M. A. Whisman (Eds.), *APA handbook of contemporary family psychology: Foundations, methods, and contemporary issues across the lifespan* (pp. 3–19). American Psychological Association. https://doi.org/10.1037/0000099-001

Fisher, P. A., & Gilliam, K. S. (2012). Multidimensional Treatment foster care: An alternative to residential treatment for high risk children and adolescents. *Intervención Psicosocial, 21*(2), 195–203. https://doi.org/10.5093/in2012a20

Flicker, S. M., Turner, C. W., Waldron, H. B., Brody, J. L., & Ozechowski, T. J. (2008). Ethnic background, therapeutic alliance, and treatment retention in functional family therapy with adolescents who abuse substances. *Journal of Family Psychology, 22*(1), 167–170. https://doi.org/10.1037/0893-3200.22.1.167

Folk, J. B., Brown, L. K., Marshall, B. D. L., Ramos, L. M. C., Gopalakrishnan, L., Koinis-Mitchell, D., & Tolou-Shams, M. (2020). The prospective impact of family functioning and parenting practices on court-involved youth's substance use and delinquent behavior. *Journal of Youth and Adolescence, 49*(1), 238–251. https://doi.org/10.1007/s10964-019-01099-8

Ford, J. D., Grasso, D. J., Hawke, J., & Chapman, J. F. (2013). Poly-victimization among juvenile justice-involved youths. *Child Abuse & Neglect, 37*(10), 788–800. https://doi.org/10.1016/j.chiabu.2013.01.005

Fowers, B. J., & Olson, D. H. (1993). ENRICH Marital satisfaction scale: A brief research and clinical tool. *Journal of Family Psychology, 7*(2), 176–185. https://doi.org/10.1037/0893-3200.7.2.176

Frick, P. J. (1991). *The Alabama Parenting Questionnaire* [Unpublished instrument]. University of Alabama. https://doi.org/10.1037/t58031-000

Friedlander, M. L., Escudero, V., & Heatherington, L. (2006). *Therapeutic alliances in couple and family therapy: An empirically informed guide to practice*. American Psychological Association. https://doi.org/10.1037/11410-000

Friedlander, M. L., Escudero, V., Welmers-van de Poll, M. J., & Heatherington, L. (2018). Meta-analysis of the alliance–outcome relation in couple and family therapy. *Psychotherapy: Theory, Research, & Practice, 55*(4), 356–371. https://doi.org/10.1037/pst0000161

Friedlander, M. L., Lee, H. H., Shaffer, K. S., & Cabrera, P. (2014). Negotiating therapeutic alliances with a family at impasse. *Psychotherapy: Theory, Research, & Practice, 51*(1), 41–52. https://doi.org/10.1037/a0032524

Gehring, K. S. (2018). A direct test of pathways theory. *Feminist Criminology, 13*(2), 115–137. https://doi.org/10.1177/1557085116646195

Gelb, A., & Velázquez, T. (2018, August 1). *The changing state of recidivism: Fewer people going back to prison*. The Pew Charitable Trusts. https://www.pewtrusts.org/en/research-and-analysis/articles/2018/08/01/the-changing-state-of-recidivism-fewer-people-going-back-to-prison

Geller, A., Cooper, C. E., Garfinkel, I., Schwartz-Soicher, O., & Mincy, R. B. (2012). Beyond absenteeism: Father incarceration and child development. *Demography, 49*(1), 49–76. https://doi.org/10.1007/s13524-011-0081-9

Ghiasi, N., Azhar, Y., & Singh, J. (2021). *Psychiatric illness and criminality*. StatPearls LLC. https://www.ncbi.nlm.nih.gov/books/NBK537064/

Glaze, L. E., & Maruschak, L. M. (2008, August). *Parents in prison and their minor children*. U.S. Department of Justice, Office of Justice Programs, Bureau of Justice Statistics. https://bjs.ojp.gov/content/pub/pdf/pptmc.pdf

Glebova, T., Foster, S. L., Cunningham, P. B., Brennan, P. A., & Whitmore, E. A. (2018). Therapists' and clients' perceptions of bonding as predictors of outcome in Multisystemic Therapy®. *Family Process, 57*(4), 867–883. https://doi.org/10.1111/famp.12333

Golder, S., Engstrom, M., Hall, M. T., Higgins, G. E., & Logan, T. K. (2015). Psychological distress among victimized women on probation and parole: A latent class analysis. *The American Journal of Orthopsychiatry, 85*(4), 382–391. https://doi.org/10.1037/ort0000057

Golder, S., Hall, M. T., Logan, T. K., Higgins, G. E., Dishon, A., Renn, T., & Winham, K. M. (2014). Substance use among victimized women on probation and parole. *Substance Use & Misuse, 49*(4), 435–447. https://doi.org/10.3109/10826084.2013.844164

Goodman, R. (1997). The Strengths and Difficulties Questionnaire: A research note. *Journal of Child Psychology and Psychiatry, and Allied Disciplines, 38*(5), 581–586. https://doi.org/10.1111/j.1469-7610.1997.tb01545.x

Goodman, R. (2001). Psychometric properties of the Strengths and Difficulties Questionnaire. *Journal of the American Academy of Child & Adolescent Psychiatry, 40*(11), 1337–1345. https://doi.org/10.1097/00004583-200111000-00015

Goorden, M., Schawo, S. J., Bouwmans-Frijters, C. A., van der Schee, E., Hendriks, V. M., & Hakkaart-van Roijen, L. (2016). The cost-effectiveness of family/family-based therapy for treatment of externalizing disorders, substance use disorders and delinquency: A systematic review. *BMC Psychiatry, 16*, 237. https://doi.org/10.1186/s12888-016-0949-8

Goorden, M., van der Schee, E., Hendriks, V. M., & Hakkaart-van Roijen, L. (2016). Cost-effectiveness of multidimensional family therapy compared to cognitive behavioral therapy for adolescents with a cannabis use disorder: Data from a randomized controlled trial. *Drug and Alcohol Dependence, 162*, 154–161. https://doi.org/10.1016/j.drugalcdep.2016.03.004

Gottfredson, D. C., Kearley, B., Thornberry, T. P., Slothower, M., Devlin, D., & Fader, J. J. (2018). Scaling-up evidence-based programs using a public funding stream: A randomized trial of functional family therapy for court-involved youth. *Prevention Science, 19*(7), 939–953. https://doi.org/10.1007/s11121-018-0936-z

Grayson, J. (2014). Juvenile justice and child protection. *Virginia Child Protection Newsletter*, 100. https://psychweb.chbs.jmu.edu/Graysojh/pdfs/Volume100.pdf

Grigorenko, E. L., Hart, L., Hein, S., Kovalenko, J., & Naumova, O. Y. (2019). Improved educational achievement as a path to desistance. *New Directions for Child and Adolescent Development, 2019*(165), 111–135. https://doi.org/10.1002/cad.20290

Hachtel, H., Vogel, T., & Huber, C. G. (2019). Mandated treatment and its impact on therapeutic process and outcome factors. *Frontiers in Psychiatry, 10*, 219. https://doi.org/10.3389/fpsyt.2019.00219

Hamilton, E., & Carr, A. (2016). Systematic review of self-report family assessment measures. *Family Process, 55*(1), 16–30. https://doi.org/10.1111/famp.12200

Harrist, A. W., Henry, C. S., Liu, C., & Sheffield Morris, A. (2019). Family resilience: The power of rituals and routines in family adaptive systems. In B. H. Fiese, M. Celano, K. Deater-Deckard, E. N. Jouriles, & M. A. Whisman (Eds.), *APA handbook of contemporary family psychology: Foundations, methods, and contemporary issues across the lifespan* (pp. 223–239). American Psychological Association. https://doi.org/10.1037/0000099-013

Hartnett, D., Carr, A., Hamilton, E., & O'Reilly, G. (2017). The effectiveness of Functional Family Therapy for adolescent behavioral and substance misuse problems: A meta-analysis. *Family Process, 56*(3), 607–619. https://doi.org/10.1111/famp.12256

Hein, S., Barbot, B., Square, A., Chapman, J., Geib, C. F., & Grigorenko, E. L. (2017). Violent offending among juveniles: A 7-year longitudinal study of recidivism, desistance, and associations with mental health. *Law and Human Behavior, 41*(3), 273–283. https://doi.org/10.1037/lhb0000241

Hendrix, J. A., & Parcel, T. L. (2014). Parental nonstandard work, family processes, and delinquency during adolescence. *Journal of Family Issues, 35*(10), 1363–1393. https://doi.org/10.1177/0192513X13510299

Henggeler, S. W., & Schaeffer, C. M. (2016). Multisystemic Therapy®: Clinical overview, outcomes, and implementation research. *Family Process, 55*(3), 514–528. https://doi.org/10.1111/famp.12232

Henggeler, S. W., & Sheidow, A. J. (2012). Empirically supported family-based treatments for conduct disorder and delinquency in adolescents. *Journal of Marital and Family Therapy, 38*(1), 30–58. https://doi.org/10.1111/j.1752-0606.2011.00244.x

Henneberger, A. K., Tolan, P. H., Hipwell, A. E., & Keenan, K. (2014). Delinquency in adolescent girls: Using a confluence approach to understand the influences of parents and peers. *Criminal Justice and Behavior, 41*(11), 1327–1337. https://doi.org/10.1177/0093854814538624

Henry, C. S., Sheffield Morris, A., & Harrist, A. W. (2015). Family resilience: Moving into the third wave. *Family Relations, 64*(1), 22–43. https://doi.org/10.1111/fare.12106

Herz, D., Lee, P., Lutz, L., Stewart, M., Tuell, J., & Wiig, J. (2012). *Addressing the needs of multi-system youth: Strengthening the connection between child welfare and juvenile justice*. Center for Juvenile Justice Reform. https://jbcc.harvard.edu/sites/default/files/addressing_the_needs_of_multi-system_youth_march_2012.pdf

Hockenberry, S. (2019). *Delinquency cases in juvenile courts, 2017*. U.S. Department of Justice, Office of Justice Programs, Office of Juvenile Justice and Delinquency Prevention. https://ojjdp.ojp.gov/sites/g/files/xyckuh176/files/media/document/253105.pdf

Hockenberry, S., & Puzzanchera, C. (2019, June). *Juvenile court statistics 2017*. National Center for Juvenile Justice. https://www.ojjdp.gov/ojstatbb/njcda/pdf/jcs2017.pdf

Hogue, A., & Liddle, H. A. (2009). Family-based treatment for adolescent substance abuse: Controlled trials and new horizons in services research. *Journal of Family Therapy, 31*(2), 126–154. https://doi.org/10.1111/j.1467-6427.2009.00459.x

Holyoak, D., Johnson, W., Garcia, M., & Johnson, D. J. (2020). I see you: Addressing diversity in clinical practice through therapist's way-of-being. *Contemporary Family Therapy, 42*(2), 131–139. https://doi.org/10.1007/s10591-019-09519-4

Holzapfel, J., Randall, A. K., Tao, C., & Iida, M. (2018). Intercultural couples' internal stress, relationship satisfaction, and dyadic coping. *Interpersona, 12*(2), 145–163. https://doi.org/10.5964/ijpr.v12i2.302

Horigian, V. E., Feaster, D. J., Brincks, A., Robbins, M. S., Perez, M. A., & Szapocznik, J. (2015). The effects of Brief Strategic Family Therapy (BSFT) on parent substance use and the association between parent and adolescent substance use. *Addictive Behaviors, 42*, 44–50. https://doi.org/10.1016/j.addbeh.2014.10.024

Horigian, V. E., Feaster, D. J., Robbins, M. S., Brincks, A. M., Ucha, J., Rohrbaugh, M. J., Shoham, V., Bachrach, K., Miller, M., Burlew, A. K., Hodgkins, C. C., Carrion, I. S., Silverstein, M., Werstlein, R., & Szapocznik, J. (2015). A cross-sectional assessment of the long term effects of Brief Strategic Family Therapy for adolescent substance use. *The American Journal on Addictions, 24*(7), 637–645. https://doi.org/10.1111/ajad.12278

Horowitz, J., & Utada, C. (2018). *Community supervision marked by racial and gender disparities*. The Pew Charitable Trusts. https://www.pewtrusts.org/

en/research-and-analysis/articles/2018/12/06/community-supervision-marked-by-racial-and-gender-disparities

Humayun, S., Herlitz, L., Chesnokov, M., Doolan, M., Landau, S., & Scott, S. (2017). Randomized controlled trial of functional family therapy for offending and antisocial behavior in UK youth. *Journal of Child Psychology and Psychiatry, 58*(9), 1023–1032. https://doi.org/10.1111/jcpp.12743

Jäggi, L. J., Mezuk, B., Watkins, D. C., & Jackson, J. S. (2016). The relationship between trauma, arrest, and incarceration history among Black Americans: Findings from the National Survey of American Life. *Society and Mental Health, 6*(3), 187–206. https://doi.org/10.1177/2156869316641730

Jérémie-Brink, G., & Chambers, A. (2019). Integrative systemic therapy with African American couples. In P. J. Pitta & C. C. Datchi (Eds.), *Integrative couple and family therapies: Treatment models for complex clinical issues* (pp. 237–255). American Psychological Association. https://doi.org/10.1037/0000151-012

Johnides, B. D., Borduin, C. M., Wagner, D. V., & Dopp, A. R. (2017). Effects of multisystemic therapy on caregivers of serious juvenile offenders: A 20-year follow-up to a randomized clinical trial. *Journal of Consulting and Clinical Psychology, 85*(4), 323–334. https://doi.org/10.1037/ccp0000199

Johnson, S. M. (2002). *Emotionally focused couple therapy with trauma survivors: Strengthening attachment bonds*. Guilford Press.

Johnson, S. M. (2003). Introduction to attachment: A therapist's guide to primary relationships and their renewal. In S. M. Johnson & V. E. Whiffen (Eds.), *Attachment processes in couple and family therapy* (pp. 3–17). Guilford Press.

Jolliffe, D., Farrington, D. P., Loeber, R., & Pardini, D. (2016). Protective factors for violence: Results from the Pittsburgh Youth Study. *Journal of Criminal Justice, 45*, 32–40. https://doi.org/10.1016/j.jcrimjus.2016.02.007

Jolliffe, D., Farrington, D. P., Piquero, A. R., Loeber, R., & Hill, K. G. (2017). Systematic review of early risk factors for life-course-persistent, adolescence-limited, and late-onset offenders in prospective longitudinal studies. *Aggression and Violent Behavior, 33*, 15–23. https://doi.org/10.1016/j.avb.2017.01.009

Jolliffe, D., Farrington, D. P., Piquero, A. R., McLeod, J. F., & van de Weijer, S. (2017). Prevalence of life-course-persistent, adolescence-limited, and late-onset offenders: A systematic review of prospective longitudinal studies. *Aggression and Violent Behavior, 33*, 4–14. https://doi.org/10.1016/j.avb.2017.01.002

Jones, A. (2018, December). *Correctional control 2018: Incarceration and supervision by state*. Prison Policy Initiative. https://www.prisonpolicy.org/reports/correctionalcontrol2018.html

Justice Center, The Council of State Governments. (2015). *Reducing recidivism and improving other outcomes for young adults in the juvenile and adult criminal justice system*. https://csgjusticecenter.org/youth/publications/reducing-recidivism-and-improving-other-outcomes-for-young-adults-in-the-juvenile-and-adult-criminal-justice-systems-2/

Kaba, F., Solimo, A., Graves, J., Glowa-Kollisch, S., Vise, A., MacDonald, R., Waters, A., Rosner, Z., Dickey, N., Angell, S., & Venters, H. (2015). Disparities in mental health referral and diagnosis in the New York City Jail Mental Health Service. *American Journal of Public Health, 105*(9), 1911–1916. https://doi.org/10.2105/AJPH.2015.302699

Kaeble, D. (2018, April). *Probation and parole in the United States, 2016*. U.S. Department of Justice, Office of Justice Programs, Bureau of Justice Statistics. https://www.bjs.gov/content/pub/pdf/ppus16.pdf

Kaeble, D., & Cowhig, M. (2018, April). *Correctional populations in the United States, 2016*. U.S. Department of Justice, Office of Justice Programs, Bureau of Justice Statistics. https://www.bjs.gov/content/pub/pdf/cpus16.pdf

Karakurt, G., Whiting, K., van Esch, C., Bolen, S. D., & Calabrese, J. R. (2016). Couples therapy for intimate partner violence: A systematic review and meta-analysis. *Journal of Marital and Family Therapy, 42*(4), 567–583. https://doi.org/10.1111/jmft.12178

Karatzias, T., Power, K., Woolston, C., Apurva, P., Begley, A., Mirza, K., Conway, L., Quinn, C., Jowett, S., Howard, R., & Purdie, A. (2018). Multiple traumatic experiences, post-traumatic stress disorder and offending behaviour in female prisoners. *Criminal Behaviour and Mental Health, 28*(1), 72–84. https://doi.org/10.1002/cbm.2043

Karlidag, E., & Morris, N. A. (2019). Social control theory. In R. Morgan (Ed.), *The Sage encyclopedia of criminal psychology* (pp. 1403–1405). Sage. https://doi.org/10.4135/9781483392240.n454

Kazura, K. (2018). Relationship intervention for inmates and their partners: Bringing couples together before release. *International Journal of Offender Therapy and Comparative Criminology, 62*(9), 2586–2600. https://doi.org/10.1177/0306624X17721525

Kennedy, T. D., Edmonds, W. A., Millen, D. H., & Detullio, D. (2019). Chronic juvenile offenders: Exploring risk factor models of recidivism. *Youth Violence and Juvenile Justice, 17*(2), 174–193. https://doi.org/10.1177/1541204018770517

Kim, K., & Peterson, B. (2014, August). *Aging behind bars: Trends and implications of aging prisoners in the federal prison system*. Urban Institute. https://www.urban.org/sites/default/files/publication/33801/413222-Aging-Behind-Bars-Trends-and-Implications-of-Graying-Prisoners-in-the-Federal-Prison-System.PDF

Kjellstrand, J., Yu, G., & Eddy, J. M. (2019). Parental incarceration as a predictor of developmental trajectories of externalizing behaviors across adolescence. *Children and Youth Services Review, 103*, 10–17. https://doi.org/10.1016/j.childyouth.2019.05.016

Kjellstrand, J., Yu, G., Eddy, J. M., Clark, M., & Jackson, A. (2020). The role of parental incarceration in predicting trajectories of child internalizing problems. *Children and Youth Services Review, 105*, 105055. https://doi.org/10.1016/j.childyouth.2020.105055

Klietz, S. J., Borduin, C. M., & Schaeffer, C. M. (2010). Cost–benefit analysis of multisystemic therapy with serious and violent juvenile offenders. *Journal of Family Psychology, 24*(5), 657–666. https://doi.org/10.1037/a0020838

Kopak, A. M., & Hoffmann, N. G. (2014). Pathways between substance use, dependence, offense type, and offense severity. *Criminal Justice Policy Review, 25*(6), 743–760. https://doi.org/10.1177/0887403413499582

Kotlaja, M., & Meier, R. F. (2019). Social bond theory. In R. Morgan (Ed.), *The Sage encyclopedia of criminal psychology* (pp. 1400–1402). Sage. https://doi.org/10.4135/9781483392240.n453

Kreis, M. K. F., Gillings, K., Svanberg, J., & Schwannauer, M. (2016). Relational pathways to substance misuse and drug-related offending in women: The role of trauma, insecure attachment, and shame. *International Journal of Forensic Mental Health, 15*(1), 35–47. https://doi.org/10.1080/14999013.2015.1134725

Krisberg, B. A., Marchionna, S., & Harney, C. J. (2019). *American corrections: Concepts and controversies* (2nd ed.). Sage.

Kroenke, K., Spitzer, R. L., & Williams, J. B. W. (2001). The PHQ–9: Validity of a brief depression severity measure. *Journal of General Internal Medicine, 16*(9), 606–613. https://doi.org/10.1046/j.1525-1497.2001.016009606.x

Krohn, M. D., Hall, G. P., & Lizotte, A. J. (2009). Family transitions and later delinquency and drug use. *Journal of Youth and Adolescence, 38*(3), 466–480. https://doi.org/10.1007/s10964-008-9366-8

Kruttschnitt, C., Joosen, K., & Bijleveld, C. (2019). Research note: Re-examining the gender responsive approach to female offending and its basis in the pathways literature. *Journal of Offender Rehabilitation, 58*(6), 485–499. https://doi.org/10.1080/10509674.2019.1621415

Kurlychek, M. C., Krohn, M. D., Dong, B., Hall, G. P., & Lizotte, A. J. (2012). Protection from risk: Exploration of when and how neighborhood-level factors can reduce violent youth outcomes. *Youth Violence and Juvenile Justice, 10*(1), 83–106. https://doi.org/10.1177/1541204011422088

Kwong Wong, S. (2017). The effects of single-mother and single-father families on youth crime: Examining five gender-related hypotheses. *International Journal of Law, Crime and Justice, 50*, 46–60. https://doi.org/10.1016/j.ijlcj.2017.04.001

Lambert, J. E., Skinner, A. H., & Friedlander, M. L. (2012). Problematic within-family alliances in conjoint family therapy: A close look at five cases. *Journal of Marital and Family Therapy, 38*(2), 417–428. https://doi.org/10.1111/j.1752-0606.2010.00212.x

Larson, M., Sweeten, G., & Piquero, A. R. (2016). With or without you? Contextualizing the impact of romantic relationship breakup on crime among serious adolescent offenders. *Journal of Youth and Adolescence, 45*(1), 54–72. https://doi.org/10.1007/s10964-015-0318-9

Latessa, E., & Lovins, B. (2012, June). *The Indiana Youth Assessment System: Final report*. University of Cincinnati, Center for Criminal Justice Research. https://www.in.gov/courts/iocs/files/prob-risk-iyas-final.pdf

LaVigne, N., Fontaine, J., & Dwivedi, A. (2017, February). *How do people in high-crime, low-income communities view the police?* Urban Institute. https://www.urban.org/sites/default/files/publication/88476/how_do_people_in_high-crime_view_the_police.pdf

Lebow, J. L. (2014). *Couple and family therapy: An integrative map of the territory.* American Psychological Association. https://doi.org/10.1037/14255-000

Lee, C. C. (2013). *Multicultural issues in counseling: New approaches to diversity* (4th ed.). American Counseling Association.

Lee, S., Aos, S., Drake, E., Pennucci, A., Miller, M., & Anderson, L. (2012, April). *Return on investment: Evidence-based options to improve statewide outcomes—April 2012 update.* (Document No. 12-04-1201). Washington State Institute for Public Policy. http://www.wsipp.wa.gov/ReportFile/1102/Wsipp_Return-on-Investment-Evidence-Based-Options-to-Improve-Statewide-Outcomes-April-2012-Update_Full-Report.pdf

Leve, L. D., Chamberlain, P., & Kim, H. K. (2015). Risks, outcomes, and evidence-based interventions for girls in the US juvenile justice system. *Clinical Child and Family Psychology Review, 18*(3), 252–279. https://doi.org/10.1007/s10567-015-0186-6

Li, S. D. (2014). Familial religiosity, family processes, and juvenile delinquency in a national sample of early adolescents. *The Journal of Early Adolescence, 34*(4), 436–462. https://doi.org/10.1177/0272431613495445

Liddle, H. A. (2014). Adapting and implementing an evidence-based treatment with justice-involved adolescents: The example of multidimensional family therapy. *Family Process, 53*(3), 516–528. https://doi.org/10.1111/famp.12094

Liddle, H. A. (2016). Multidimensional family therapy. In T. L. Sexton & J. Lebow (Eds.), *Handbook of family therapy* (pp. 231–249). Routledge.

Liddle, H. A., Dakof, G. A., Henderson, C., & Rowe, C. (2011). Implementation outcomes of multidimensional family therapy–detention to community: A reintegration program for drug-using juvenile detainees. *International Journal of Offender Therapy and Comparative Criminology, 55*(4), 587–604. https://doi.org/10.1177/0306624X10366960

Liddle, H. A., Dakof, G. A., Parker, K., Diamond, G. S., Barrett, K., & Tejeda, M. (2001). Multidimensional family therapy for adolescent drug abuse: Results of a randomized clinical trial. *The American Journal of Drug and Alcohol Abuse, 27*(4), 651–688. https://doi.org/10.1081/ADA-100107661

Liddle, H. A., Dakof, G. A., Rowe, C. L., Henderson, C., Greenbaum, P., Wang, W., & Alberga, L. (2018). Multidimensional family therapy as a community-based alternative to residential treatment for adolescents with substance use and co-occurring mental health disorders. *Journal of Substance Abuse Treatment, 90*, P47–P56. https://doi.org/10.1016/j.jsat.2018.04.011

Lilliott, E. A., Trott, E. M., Kellett, N. C., Green, A. E., & Willging, C. E. (2017). Women, incarceration and reentry: The revolving door of prisons. In C. C. Datchi & J. Ancis (Eds.), *Gender, psychology, and justice: The mental health of women and girls in the legal system* (pp. 127–150). New York University Press. https://doi.org/10.18574/nyu/9781479819850.003.0006

Limoncelli, K. E., Wolff, K. T., & Celinska, K. (2019). The role of parental problems in functional family therapy outcomes. *Children and Youth Services Review, 106*, 104483. https://doi.org/10.1016/j.childyouth.2019.104483

Lindstrøm, M., Filges, T., & Jørgensen, A.-M. K. (2015). Brief strategic family therapy for young people in treatment for drug use. *Research on Social Work Practice, 25*(1), 61–80. https://doi.org/10.1177/1049731514530003

Linhof, A. Y., & Allan, R. (2019). A narrative expansion of emotionally focused therapy with intercultural couples. *The Family Journal, 27*(1), 44–49. https://doi.org/10.1177/1066480718809426

Lippold, M. A., Hussong, A., Fosco, G. M., & Ram, N. (2018). Lability in the parent's hostility and warmth toward their adolescent: Linkages to youth delinquency and substance use. *Developmental Psychology, 54*(2), 348–361. https://doi.org/10.1037/dev0000415

Locke, H. J., & Wallace, K. M. (1959). Short marital-adjustment and prediction tests: Their reliability and validity. *Marriage and Family Living, 21*(3), 251–255. https://doi.org/10.2307/348022

Loeber, R., Farrington, D. P., & Petechuk, D. (2014, March 10). *From juvenile delinquency to young adult offending*. National Institute of Justice. https://nij.ojp.gov/topics/articles/juvenile-delinquency-young-adult-offending

Looman, J., & Abracen, J. (2013). The risk need responsivity model of offender rehabilitation: Is there really a need for paradigm shift? *International Journal of Behavioral and Consultation Therapy, 8*(3–4), 30–36. https://doi.org/10.1037/h0100980

Looney, A., & Turner, N. (2018, March 14). *Work and opportunity before and after incarceration*. The Brookings Institution. https://www.brookings.edu/research/work-and-opportunity-before-and-after-incarceration/

Low, S., Sinclair, R., & Shortt, J. W. (2012). The role of economic strain on adolescent delinquency: A microsocial process model. *Journal of Family Psychology, 26*(4), 576–584. https://doi.org/10.1037/a0028785

Lucero, J. L., Barrett, C., & Jensen, H. (2015). An examination of family and school factors related to early delinquency. *Children & Schools, 37*(3), 165–173. https://doi.org/10.1093/cs/cdv013

Lynch, S. M., DeHart, D. D., Belknap, J., & Green, B. L. (2012). *Women's pathways to jail: The roles and intersections of serious mental illness and trauma*. Bureau of Justice Assistance, U.S. Department of Justice. https://bja.ojp.gov/sites/g/files/xyckuh186/files/Publications/Women_Pathways_to_Jail.pdf

Lynch, S. M., DeHart, D. D., Belknap, J., & Green, B. L. (2013, March). *Women's pathways to jail: Examining mental health, trauma, and substance use*. U.S. Department of Justice, Office of Justice Programs, Bureau of Justice Assistance. https://bja.ojp.gov/sites/g/files/xyckuh186/files/Publications/WomensPathwaysToJail.pdf

Lyngstad, T. H., & Skardhamar, T. (2013). Changes in criminal offending around the time of marriage. *Journal of Research in Crime and Delinquency, 50*(4), 608–615. https://doi.org/10.1177/0022427812469516

Mack, K. Y., Leiber, M. J., Featherstone, R. A., & Monserud, M. A. (2007). Reassessing the family–delinquency association: Do family type, family processes, and economic factors make a difference? *Journal of Criminal Justice, 35*(1), 51–67. https://doi.org/10.1016/j.jcrimjus.2006.11.015

Maeschalck, C. L., & Barfknecht, L. R. (2017). Using client feedback to inform treatment. In D. S. Prescott, C. L. Maeschalck, & S. D. Miller (Eds.), *Feedback-informed treatment in clinical practice: Reaching for excellence* (pp. 53–77). American Psychological Association. https://doi.org/10.1037/0000039-004

Mansfield, A. K., Keitner, G. I., & Sheeran, T. (2019). The Brief Assessment of Family Functioning Scale (BAFFS): A three-item version of the General Functioning Scale of the Family Assessment Device. *Psychotherapy Research, 29*(6), 824–831. https://doi.org/10.1080/10503307.2017.1422213

Martin, E. (2017, March 1). Hidden consequences: The impact of incarceration on dependent children. *National Institute of Justice Journal, 278*, 1–7. https://nij.ojp.gov/topics/articles/hidden-consequences-impact-incarceration-dependent-children

Maschi, T. (2006). Unraveling the link between trauma and male delinquency: The cumulative versus differential risk perspectives. *Social Work, 51*(1), 59–70. https://doi.org/10.1093/sw/51.1.59

Mauer, M., & King, R. S. (2007). *A 25-year quagmire: The war on drugs and its impact on American society*. The Sentencing Project. https://www.sentencingproject.org/wp-content/uploads/2016/01/A-25-Year-Quagmire-The-War-On-Drugs-and-Its-Impact-on-American-Society.pdf

McFarlane, W. R., & Cook, W. L. (2007). Family expressed emotion prior to onset of psychosis. *Family Process, 46*(2), 185–197. https://doi.org/10.1111/j.1545-5300.2007.00203.x

McGoldrick, M., & Ashton, D. (2012). Culture: A challenge to concepts of normality. In F. Walsh (Ed.), *Normal family processes: Growing diversity and complexity* (4th ed., pp. 249–272). Guilford Press.

McGoldrick, M., Gerson, R., & Petry, S. (2020). *Genograms: Assessment and treatment* (4th ed.). W. W. Norton.

McKee, S. A., & Hilton, N. Z. (2019). Co-occurring substance use, PTSD, and IPV victimization: Implications for female offender services. *Trauma, Violence & Abuse, 20*(3), 303–314. https://doi.org/10.1177/1524838017708782

Mears, D. P., & Cochran, J. C. (2015). *Prisoner reentry in the era of mass incarceration*. Sage. https://doi.org/10.4135/9781483390727

Meldrum, R. C., Connolly, G. M., Flexon, J., & Guerette, R. T. (2016). Parental low self-control, family environments, and juvenile delinquency. *International Journal of Offender Therapy and Comparative Criminology, 60*(14), 1623–1644. https://doi.org/10.1177/0306624X15584907

Miller, A. L., Perryman, J., Markovitz, L., Franzen, S., Cochran, S., & Brown, S. (2013). Strengthening incarcerated families: Evaluating a pilot program for children of incarcerated parents and their caregivers. *Family Relations, 62*(4), 584–596. https://doi.org/10.1111/fare.12029

Miller, J. K., Todahl, J. L., & Platt, J. J. (2010). The core competency movement in marriage and family therapy: Key considerations from other disciplines. *Journal of Marital and Family Therapy, 36*(1), 59–70. https://doi.org/10.1111/j.1752-0606.2009.00183.x

Miller, J. M., Miller, H. V., & Barnes, J. C. (2016). Outcome evaluation of a family-based jail reentry program for substance abusing offenders. *The Prison Journal, 96*(1), 53–78. https://doi.org/10.1177/0032885515605482

Minuchin, S. (1974). *Families and family therapy*. Harvard University Press.

Moos, R. H. (2009). *Family Environment Scale manual and sampler set: Development, applications and research*. Mind Garden.

Morenoff, J. D., & Harding, D. J. (2014). Incarceration, prisoner reentry, and communities. *Annual Review of Sociology, 40*(1), 411–429. https://doi.org/10.1146/annurev-soc-071811-145511

Mowen, T. J., & Boman, J. H., IV. (2018). A developmental perspective on reentry: Understanding the causes and consequences of family conflict and peer delinquency during adolescence and emerging adulthood. *Journal of Youth and Adolescence, 47*(2), 275–289. https://doi.org/10.1007/s10964-017-0794-1

MultiDimensional Family Therapy. (n.d.). *Certification*. https://www.mdft.org/certification

Mulvey, E. P., Schubert, C. A., & Chassin, L. (2010, December). Substance use and delinquent behavior among serious adolescent offenders. *Juvenile Justice Bulletin*. https://www.ncjrs.gov/pdffiles1/ojjdp/232790.pdf

Murray, J., Farrington, D. P., & Sekol, I. (2012). Children's antisocial behavior, mental health, drug use, and educational performance after parental incarceration: A systematic review and meta-analysis. *Psychological Bulletin, 138*(2), 175–210. https://doi.org/10.1037/a0026407

National Association of Drug Court Professionals. (n.d.). *Drug courts in the US: Cutting crime, saving money*. https://www.nadcp.org/wp-content/uploads/2018/11/US-Drug-Court-Fact-Sheet-2018.pdf

National Criminal Justice Reference Service. (2017). *Crime trends*. https://www.ncjrs.gov/ovc_archives/ncvrw/2017/images/en_artwork/Fact_Sheets/2017NCVRW_CrimeTrends_508.pdf

National Drug Court Resource Center. (n.d.). *National drug court database and map*. https://ndcrc.org/maps/

National Institute of Corrections. (2004). *Implementing evidence-based practice in community corrections: The principles of effective interventions*. https://nicic.gov/implementing-evidence-based-practice-community-corrections-principles-effective-intervention

National Institute of Justice. (n.d.-a). *Rated programs*. https://www.crimesolutions.gov/Programs.aspx#view-programs

National Institute of Justice. (n.d.-b). *Recidivism*. https://nij.ojp.gov/topics/corrections/recidivism

National Institute of Justice. (2020). *Practice profile: Rehabilitation programs for adult offenders*. https://crimesolutions.ojp.gov/ratedpractices/101

National Institute on Drug Abuse. (2019). *DrugFacts: Criminal justice*. https://www.drugabuse.gov/publications/drugfacts/criminal-justice

National Research Council. (2014). *The growth of incarceration in the United States: Exploring causes and consequences*. https://nicic.gov/growth-incarceration-united-states-exploring-causes-and-consequences

National Research Council & Institute of Medicine. (2001). *Juvenile crime, juvenile justice*. National Academies Press. https://doi.org/10.17226/9747

Nelson, L., & Lind, D. (2015, October 27). *The school-to-prison pipeline, explained*. http://www.justicepolicy.org/news/8775

Office of Juvenile Justice and Delinquency Prevention. (n.d.-a). *Delinquency cases*. https://www.ojjdp.gov/ojstatbb/court/qa06201.asp?qaDate=2017

Office of Juvenile Justice and Delinquency Prevention. (n.d.-b). *Trends and characteristics of youth in residential placement, 2017*. https://www.ojjdp.gov/ojstatbb/snapshots/DataSnapshot_CJRP2017.pdf

Office of Juvenile Justice and Delinquency Prevention. (1997). *Balanced and restorative justice for juveniles: A framework for juvenile justice in the 21st century*. https://www.ncjrs.gov/pdffiles/framwork.pdf

Office of Juvenile Justice and Delinquency Prevention. (1999). *Juvenile justice: A century of change*. https://www.ncjrs.gov/pdffiles1/ojjdp/178995.pdf

Office of Juvenile Justice and Delinquency Prevention. (2016). *Juvenile justice system structure and process: Organization and administration of delinquency services*. https://www.ojjdp.gov/ojstatbb/structure_process/qa04205.asp?qaDate=2016

Office of Juvenile Justice and Delinquency Prevention. (2017a, July). *Intersection between mental health and juvenile justice system*. https://www.ojjdp.gov/mpg/litreviews/Intersection-Mental-Health-Juvenile-Justice.pdf

Office of Juvenile Justice and Delinquency Prevention. (2017b, August). *Aftercare services*. https://www.ojjdp.gov/mpg/litreviews/Aftercare.pdf

Office of Juvenile Justice and Delinquency Prevention. (2019). *Statistical briefing book*. https://www.ojjdp.gov/ojstatbb/

Office of the Surgeon General. (2001). *Mental health: Culture, race, and ethnicity: A supplement to* Mental health: A report of the Surgeon General. Substance Abuse and Mental Health Services Administration. https://www.ncbi.nlm.nih.gov/books/NBK44246/

Ofonedu, M. E., Belcher, H. M. E., Budhathoki, C., & Gross, D. A. (2017). Understanding barriers to initial treatment engagement among underserved families seeking mental health services. *Journal of Child and Family Studies, 26*(3), 863–876. https://doi.org/10.1007/s10826-016-0603-6

O'Keeffe, S., Martin, P., Target, M., & Midgley, N. (2019). "I just stopped going": A mixed methods investigation into types of therapy dropout in adolescents with depression. *Frontiers in Psychology*, *10*(10), 75. https://doi.org/10.3389/fpsyg.2019.00075

Olson, D. (2011). FACES IV and the circumplex model: Validation study. *Journal of Marital and Family Therapy*, *37*(1), 64–80. https://doi.org/10.1111/j.1752-0606.2009.00175.x

Olson, D. H., & Gorall, D. M. (2003). Circumplex model of marital and family systems. In F. Walsh (Ed.), *Normal family processes: Growing diversity and complexity* (3rd ed., pp. 514–548). Guilford Press.

Olver, M. E., Stockdale, K. C., & Wormith, J. S. (2011). A meta-analysis of predictors of offender treatment attrition and its relationship to recidivism. *Journal of Consulting and Clinical Psychology*, *79*(1), 6–21. https://doi.org/10.1037/a0022200

Osher, F., D'Amora, D. A., Plotkin, M., Jarrett, N., & Eggleston, A. (2012). *Adults with behavioral health needs under correctional supervision: A shared framework for reducing recidivism and promoting recovery.* The Council of State Governments Justice Center. https://bja.ojp.gov/sites/g/files/xyckuh186/files/Publications/CSG_Behavioral_Framework.pdf

The Pew Center on the States. (2011, April). *State of recidivism: The revolving door of America's prisons.* http://www.pewtrusts.org/~/media/legacy/uploadedfiles/pcs_assets/2011/pewstateofrecidivismpdf.pdf

The Pew Charitable Trusts. (2010). *Collateral costs: Incarceration's effect on economic mobility*. https://www.pewtrusts.org/~/media/legacy/uploadedfiles/pcs_assets/2010/collateralcosts1pdf.pdf

The Pew Charitable Trusts. (2018, September). *Probation and parole systems marked by high stakes, missed opportunities*. https://www.pewtrusts.org/-/media/assets/2018/09/probation_and_parole_systems_marked_by_high_stakes_missed_opportunities_pew.pdf

The Pew Charitable Trusts. (2019, July). *To safely cut incarceration, states rethink responses to supervision violations*. https://www.pewtrusts.org/-/media/assets/2019/07/pspp_states_target_technical_violations_v1.pdf

Pinsof, W. M., Goldsmith, J. Z., & Latta, T. A. (2012). Information technology and feedback research can bridge the scientist–practitioner gap: A couple therapy example. *Couple & Family Psychology*, *1*(4), 253–273. https://doi.org/10.1037/a0031023

Piquero, A. R., Jennings, W. G., Diamond, B., Farrington, D. P., Tremblay, R. E., Welsh, B. C., & Gonzalez, J. M. R. (2016). A meta-analysis update on the effects of early family/parent training programs on antisocial behavior and delinquency. *Journal of Experimental Criminology*, *12*(2), 229–248. https://doi.org/10.1007/s11292-016-9256-0

Pitta, P. J., & Datchi, C. C. (Eds.). (2019). *Integrative couple and family therapies: Treatment models for complex clinical issues*. American Psychological Association. https://doi.org/10.1037/0000151-000

Pope, L. (2019, July 24). *Racial disparities in mental health and criminal justice*. https://www.nami.org/Blogs/NAMI-Blog/July-2019/Racial-Disparities-in-Mental-Health-and-Criminal-Justice

Rathgeber, M., Bürkner, P. C., Schiller, E. M., & Holling, H. (2019). The efficacy of emotionally focused couples therapy and behavioral couples therapy: A meta-analysis. *Journal of Marital and Family Therapy, 45*(3), 447–463. https://doi.org/10.1111/jmft.12336

Ratts, M. J., Singh, A. A., Nassar-McMillan, S., Butler, S. K., & McCullough, J. R. (2016). Multicultural and social justice counseling competencies: Guidelines for the counseling profession. *Journal of Multicultural Counseling and Development, 44*(1), 28–48. https://doi.org/10.1002/jmcd.12035

Repetti, R. L., & Saxbe, D. E. (2019). The influence of chronic family stressors on adult health. In B. H. Fiese, M. Celano, K. Deater-Deckard, E. N. Jouriles, & M. A. Whisman (Eds.), *APA handbook of contemporary family psychology: Vol. 2. Foundations, methods, and contemporary issues across the lifespan* (pp. 121–136). American Psychological Association. https://doi.org/10.1037/0000100-008

Rhoades, K. A., Leve, L. D., Eddy, J. M., & Chamberlain, P. (2016). Predicting the transition from juvenile delinquency to adult criminality: Gender-specific influences in two high-risk samples. *Criminal Behaviour and Mental Health, 26*(5), 336–351. https://doi.org/10.1002/cbm.1957

Rifkin, L. (2017). Barbarous and ineffective: A blueprint for challenging criminalization of people with mental illnesses and psychiatric disabilities. *UCLA Criminal Justice Law Review, 1*(1), 57–76. https://escholarship.org/uc/item/90z1m06b

Robbins, M. S., Feaster, D. J., Horigian, V. E., Rohrbaugh, M., Shoham, V., Bachrach, K., Miller, M., Burlew, K. A., Hodgkins, C., Carrion, I., Vandermark, N., Schindler, E., Werstlein, R., & Szapocznik, J. (2011). Brief strategic family therapy versus treatment as usual: Results of a multisite randomized trial for substance using adolescents. *Journal of Consulting and Clinical Psychology, 79*(6), 713–727. https://doi.org/10.1037/a0025477

Rocque, M., Posick, C., Barkan, S. E., & Paternoster, R. (2015). Marriage and county-level crime rates: A research note. *Journal of Research in Crime and Delinquency, 52*(1), 130–145. https://doi.org/10.1177/0022427814547113

Roddy, M. K., Walsh, L. M., Rothman, K., Hatch, S. G., & Doss, B. D. (2020). Meta-analysis of couple therapy: Effects across outcomes, designs, timeframes, and other moderators. *Journal of Consulting and Clinical Psychology, 88*(7), 583–596. https://doi.org/10.1037/ccp0000514

Roos, J., & Werbart, A. (2013). Therapist and relationship factors influencing dropout from individual psychotherapy: A literature review. *Psychotherapy Research, 23*(4), 394–418. https://doi.org/10.1080/10503307.2013.775528

Rowe, C. L. (2010). Multidimensional family therapy: Addressing co-occurring substance abuse and other problems among adolescents with comprehensive family-based treatment. *Child and Adolescent Psychiatric Clinics of North America, 19*(3), 563–576. https://doi.org/10.1016/j.chc.2010.03.008

Rubens, S. L., Gudiño, O. G., Michel, J., Fite, P. J., & Johnson-Motoyama, M. (2018). Neighborhood and cultural stressors associated with delinquency in Latino adolescents. *Journal of Community Psychology, 46*(1), 95–106. https://doi.org/10.1002/jcop.21918

Rubin, N. J., Bebeau, M., Leigh, I. W., Lichtenberg, J. W., Nelson, P. D., Portnoy, S., Smith, I. L., & Kaslow, N. J. (2007). The competency movement within psychology: An historical perspective. *Professional Psychology: Research and Practice, 38*(5), 452–462. https://doi.org/10.1037/0735-7028.38.5.452

Ryan, C. E., Epstein, N., Keitner, G., Miller, I., & Bishop, D. (2005). *Evaluating and treating families: The McMaster approach*. Routledge. https://doi.org/10.4324/9780203843840

Sabol, W. J., Johnson, T. L., & Caccavale, A. (2019, December). *Trends in correctional control by race and sex. Council on Criminal Justice*. https://www.ncsl.org/Portals/1/Documents/cj/advancing-justice/Council%20on%20Criminal%20Justice%20Trends.pdf

Saldana, L., Campbell, M., Leve, L., & Chamberlain, P. (2019). Long-term economic benefit of Treatment Foster Care Oregon (TFCO) for adolescent females referred to congregate care for delinquency. *Child Welfare, 97*(5), 179–195.

Saloner, B., & Lê Cook, B. (2013). Blacks and Hispanics are less likely than whites to complete addiction treatment, largely due to socioeconomic factors. *Health Affairs, 32*(1), 135–145. https://doi.org/10.1377/hlthaff.2011.0983

Sampson, R. J., Laub, J. H., & Wimer, C. (2006). Does marriage reduce crime? A counterfactual approach to within-individual causal effects. *Criminology, 44*(3), 465–508. https://doi.org/10.1111/j.1745-9125.2006.00055.x

Sanders, J., Hershberger, A. R., Kolp, H. M., Um, M., Aalsma, M., & Cyders, M. A. (2018). PTSD symptoms mediate the relationship between sexual abuse and substance use risk in juvenile justice–involved youth. *Child Maltreatment, 23*(3), 226–233. https://doi.org/10.1177/1077559517745154

Savolainen, J., Eisman, A., Mason, W. A., Schwartz, J. A., Miettunen, J., & Järvelin, M. R. (2018). Socioeconomic disadvantage and psychological deficits: Pathways from early cumulative risk to late-adolescent criminal conviction. *Journal of Adolescence, 65*, 16–24. https://doi.org/10.1016/j.adolescence.2018.02.010

Sawyer, A. M., & Borduin, C. M. (2011). Effects of multisystemic therapy through midlife: A 21.9-year follow-up to a randomized clinical trial with serious and violent juvenile offenders. *Journal of Consulting and Clinical Psychology, 79*(5), 643–652. https://doi.org/10.1037/a0024862

Schoenwald, S. K., Henggeler, S. W., & Rowland, M. D. (2016). Multisystemic therapy. In T. L. Sexton & J. Lebow (Eds.), *Handbook of family therapy* (pp. 271–285). Routledge/Taylor & Francis.

Schubert, C. A., & Mulvey, E. P. (2014, June). Behavioral health problems, treatment and outcomes in serious youthful offenders. *Juvenile Justice Bulletin*. https://www.pathwaysstudy.pitt.edu/documents/Behavioral%20Health%20Problem,%20Treatment%20and%20Outcomes%20in%20Serious%20Youthful%20Offenders.pdf

Scott, C. K., Grella, C. E., Dennis, M. L., & Funk, R. R. (2016). A time-varying model of risk for predicting recidivism among women offenders over 3 years following their release from jail. *Criminal Justice and Behavior, 43*(9), 1137–1158. https://doi.org/10.1177/0093854816632551

Scott, C. L. (2010). *Handbook of correctional mental health* (2nd ed.). American Psychiatric Association.

Scruggs, S. M., Meyer, R., & Kayo, R. (2014). *Community Reinforcement and Family Training: Support and Prevention (CRAFT-SP)*. https://www.mirecc.va.gov/visn16/docs/CRAFT-SP_Final.pdf

The Sentencing Project. (2021, May 17). *Fact sheet: Trends in U.S. corrections*. https://www.sentencingproject.org/publications/trends-in-u-s-corrections/

Sexton, T., & Turner, C. W. (2010). The effectiveness of functional family therapy for youth with behavioral problems in a community practice setting. *Journal of Family Psychology, 24*(3), 339–348. https://doi.org/10.1037/a0019406

Sexton, T. L. (n.d.). *Functional family therapy*. https://www1.nyc.gov/assets/acs/pdf/RFP/2019/FFTAssociatesHandouts.pdf

Sexton, T. L. (2011). *Functional family therapy in clinical practice: An evidence-based treatment model for working with troubled adolescents*. Routledge. https://doi.org/10.4324/9780203882665

Sexton, T. L. (2016). Functional family therapy: Evidence-based and clinically creative. In T. L. Sexton & J. Lebow (Eds.), *Handbook of family therapy* (pp. 250–270). Routledge.

Sexton, T. L., Datchi, C., Evans, L., LaFollette, J., & Wright, L. (2013). The effectiveness of couple and family-based clinical interventions. In M. J. Lambert (Ed.), *Bergin and Garfield's handbook of psychotherapy and behavior change* (6th ed., pp. 587–639). Wiley.

Sexton, T. L., & Fisher, A. (2016). Integrating ongoing measurement into the clinical decision-making process with measurement feedback systems. In J. J. Magnavita (Ed.), *Clinical decision making in mental health practice* (pp. 223–244). American Psychological Association. https://doi.org/10.1037/14711-009

Sexton, T. L., Patterson, T., & Datchi, C. C. (2012). Technological innovations of systematic measurement and clinical feedback: A virtual leap into the future of couple and family psychology. *Couple & Family Psychology, 1*(4), 285–293. https://doi.org/10.1037/cfp0000001

Sexton, T. L., Ridley, C. R., & Kleiner, A. J. (2004). Beyond common factors: Multilevel-process models of therapeutic change in marriage and family therapy. *Journal of Marital and Family Therapy, 30*(2), 131–149. https://doi.org/10.1111/j.1752-0606.2004.tb01229.x

Shadish, W. R., & Baldwin, S. A. (2003). Meta-analysis of MFT interventions. *Journal of Marital and Family Therapy, 29*(4), 547–570. https://doi.org/10.1111/j.1752-0606.2003.tb01694.x

Shadish, W. R., Ragsdale, K., Glaser, R. R., & Montgomery, L. M. (1995). The efficacy and effectiveness of marital and family therapy: A perspective from meta-analysis. *Journal of Marital and Family Therapy, 21*(4), 345–360. https://doi.org/10.1111/j.1752-0606.1995.tb00170.x

Shamblen, S. R., Arnold, B. B., McKiernan, P., Collins, D. A., & Strader, T. N. (2013). Applying the creating lasting family connections marriage enhancement program to marriages affected by prison reentry. *Family Process, 52*(3), 477–498. https://doi.org/10.1111/famp.12003

Sheehan, A. H., & Friedlander, M. L. (2015). Therapeutic alliance and retention in brief strategic family therapy: A mixed-methods study. *Journal of Marital and Family Therapy*, *41*(4), 415–427. https://doi.org/10.1111/jmft.12113

Sickmund, M., & Puzzanchera, C. (2014). *Juvenile offenders and victims: 2014 national report*. National Center for Juvenile Justice. https://www.ojjdp.gov/ojstatbb/nr2014/downloads/chapter6.pdf

Simmons, C., Steinberg, L., Frick, P. J., & Cauffman, E. (2018). The differential influence of absent and harsh fathers on juvenile delinquency. *Journal of Adolescence*, *62*, 9–17. https://doi.org/10.1016/j.adolescence.2017.10.010

Sinclair, I., Parry, E., Biehal, N., Fresen, J., Kay, C., Scott, S., & Green, J. (2016). Multi-dimensional treatment foster care in England: Differential effects by level of initial antisocial behaviour. *European Child & Adolescent Psychiatry*, *25*(8), 843–852. https://doi.org/10.1007/s00787-015-0799-9

Singh, A. A., Nassar, S. C., Arredondo, P., & Toporek, R. (2020). The past guides the future: Implementing the multicultural and social justice counseling competencies. *Journal of Counseling and Development*, *98*(3), 238–252. https://doi.org/10.1002/jcad.12319

Skinner, H. A., Steinhauer, P. D., & Santa-Barbara, J. (2000). *The Family Assessment Measure III™*. https://storefront.mhs.com/collections/fam-iii

Smith, C. J., & Young, D. S. (2017). A retrospective look at the experience of parental incarceration and family reentry during adolescence. *Social Work in Public Health*, *32*(8), 475–488. https://doi.org/10.1080/19371918.2017.1360819

Smith, E. P., Faulk, M., & Sizer, M. A. (2016). Exploring the meso-system: The roles of community, family, and peers in adolescent delinquency and positive youth development. *Youth & Society*, *48*(3), 318–343. https://doi.org/10.1177/0044118X13491581

Snyder, D. K. (1997). *Manual for the Marital Satisfaction Inventory–Revised*. Western Psychological Services.

Snyder, H. N. (2012). *Arrest in the United States, 1990–2010*. U.S. Department of Justice, Office of Justice Programs, Bureau of Justice Statistics. https://bjs.ojp.gov/content/pub/pdf/aus9010.pdf

Snyder, J., & Stoolmiller, M. (2002). Reinforcement and coercion mechanisms in the development of antisocial behavior: The family. In J. B. Reid, G. R. Patterson, & J. Snyder (Eds.), *Antisocial behavior in children and adolescents: A developmental analysis and model for intervention* (pp. 65–100). American Psychological Association. https://doi.org/10.1037/10468-004

Solomon, B. J., Davis, L. E. G., & Luckham, B. (2012). The relationship between trauma and delinquent decision making among adolescent female offenders: Mediating effects. *Journal of Child & Adolescent Trauma*, *5*(2), 161–172. https://doi.org/10.1080/19361521.2012.672546

Sotero, L., Cunha, D., da Silva, J. T., Escudero, V., & Relvas, A. P. (2017). Building alliances with (in)voluntary clients: A study focused on therapists' observable behaviors. *Family Process, 56*(4), 819–834. https://doi.org/10.1111/famp.12265

Spanier, G. B. (1976). Measuring dyadic adjustment: New scales for assessing the quality of marriage and similar dyads. *Journal of Marriage and the Family, 38*(1), 15–28. https://doi.org/10.2307/350547

Sperry, L. (Ed.). (2011). *Family assessment: Contemporary and cutting-edge strategies* (2nd ed.). Routledge.

Sprenkle, D. H., Davis, S. D., & Lebow, J. L. (2009). *Common factors in couple and family therapy: The overlooked foundation for effective practice*. Guilford Press.

Stanton, M. (2009). The systemic epistemology of the specialty of family psychology. In J. H. Bray & M. Stanton (Eds.), *The Wiley-Blackwell handbook of family psychology* (pp. 5–20). Wiley-Blackwell. https://doi.org/10.1002/9781444310238.ch1

Stanton, M., & Welsh, R. (2011). *Specialty competencies in couple and family psychology*. Oxford University Press. https://doi.org/10.1093/med:psych/9780195387872.001.0001

Stevens, M. (2018). Preventing at-risk children from developing antisocial and criminal behaviour: A longitudinal study examining the role of parenting, community and societal factors in middle childhood. *BMC Psychology, 6*(1), 40. https://doi.org/10.1186/s40359-018-0254-z

Strong, S. M., Rantala, R. R., & Kyckelhahn, T. (2016). *Census of problem solving courts, 2012*. U.S. Department of Justice, Office of Justice Programs, Bureau of Justice Statistics. https://www.bjs.gov/index.cfm?ty=pbdetail&iid=5744

Substance Abuse and Mental Health Services Administration. (2014, March 6). *Trends in substance use disorders among males aged 18 to 49 on probation or parole*. https://www.samhsa.gov/data/sites/default/files/sr084-males-probation-parole/sr084-males-probation-parole/sr084-males-probation-parole.htm

Swift, J. K., & Greenberg, R. P. (2012). Premature discontinuation in adult psychotherapy: A meta-analysis. *Journal of Consulting and Clinical Psychology, 80*(4), 547–559. https://doi.org/10.1037/a0028226

Szapocznik, J., Hervis, O., & Schwartz, S. (2003). *Brief strategic family therapy for adolescent drug abuse*. https://doi.org/10.1037/e598162007-001

Szapocznik, J., Huff, J. H., Schwartz, S. J., Muir, J. A., & Hendricks Brown, C. (2016). Brief strategic family therapy treatment for behavior problem youth. In T. L. Sexton & J. Lebow (Eds.), *Handbook of family therapy* (pp. 286–304). Routledge.

Szapocznik, J., Muir, J. A., Duff, J. H., Schwartz, S. J., & Brown, C. H. (2015). Brief strategic family therapy: Implementing evidence-based models in community settings. *Psychotherapy Research, 25*(1), 121–133. https://doi.org/10.1080/10503307.2013.856044

Taylor, E. K., & Borduin, C. M. (2014). The family context of relational aggression in "difficult to treat" female juvenile offenders. *Journal of Marital and Family Therapy, 40*(3), 357–366. https://doi.org/10.1111/jmft.12038

Teplin, L. A., Welty, L. J., Abram, K. M., Dulcan, M. K., Washburn, J. J., McCoy, K., & Stockes, M. L. (2015, September). Psychiatric disorders in youth after detention. *Juvenile Justice Bulletin*. https://ojjdp.ojp.gov/sites/g/files/xyckuh176/files/pubs/246824.pdf

Theobald, D., Farrington, D. P., & Piquero, A. R. (2013). Childhood broken homes and adult violence: An analysis of moderators and mediators. *Journal of Criminal Justice, 41*(1), 44–52. https://doi.org/10.1016/j.jcrimjus.2012.12.003

Thomlison, B. (2016). *Family assessment handbook: An introduction and practical guide to family assessment* (4th ed.). Cengage Learning.

Thompson, C. M., Datchi, C. C., & Eure, L. (in press). Taking back the streets: Violence prevention and neighborhood empowerment in the South Ward of Newark. In C. C. Clauss-Ehlers (Ed.), *The Cambridge handbook of community psychology*. Cambridge University Press.

Thompson, S. J., Bender, K., Lantry, J., & Flynn, P. M. (2007). Treatment engagement: Building therapeutic alliance in home-based treatment with adolescents and their families. *Contemporary Family Therapy, 29*(1–2), 39–55. https://doi.org/10.1007/s10591-007-9030-6

Tofig, D. (2017, January 11). *Education and training opportunities in America's prisons*. National Center for Education Statistics. https://nces.ed.gov/blogs/nces/2017/01/11/default

Tolou-Shams, M., Brogan, L., Esposito-Smythers, C., Healy, M. G., Lowery, A., Craker, L., & Brown, L. K. (2018). The role of family functioning in parenting practices of court-involved youth. *Journal of Adolescence, 63*, 165–174. https://doi.org/10.1016/j.adolescence.2017.12.016

Tolou-Shams, M., Yonek, J., Galbraith, K., & Bath, E. (2019). Text messaging to enhance behavioral health treatment engagement among justice-involved youth: Qualitative and user testing study. *JMIR mHealth and uHealth, 7*(4), e10904. https://doi.org/10.2196/10904

Tuerk, E. H., McCart, M. R., & Henggeler, S. W. (2012). Collaboration in family therapy. *Journal of Clinical Psychology, 68*(2), 168–178. https://doi.org/10.1002/jclp.21833

Turney, K., & Goodsell, R. (2018). Parental incarceration and children's well-being. *The Future of Children, 28*(1), 147–164. https://doi.org/10.1353/foc.2018.0007

U.S. Department of Education Office for Civil Rights. (2014, March). *Civil rights data collection: Data snapshot. School discipline*. https://www2.ed.gov/about/offices/list/ocr/docs/crdc-discipline-snapshot.pdf

U.S. Department of Justice. (2009, December 1). *Addressing mental illness in the criminal justice system*. https://www.justice.gov/archives/opa/blog/addressing-mental-illness-criminal-justice-system

Valdez, A., Cepeda, A., Parrish, D., Horowitz, R., & Kaplan, C. (2013). An adapted brief strategic family therapy for gang-affiliated Mexican American adolescents. *Research on Social Work Practice, 23*(4), 383–396. https://doi.org/10.1177/1049731513481389

van der Pol, T. M., Henderson, C. E., Hendriks, V., Schaub, M. P., & Rigter, H. (2018). Multidimensional family therapy reduces self-reported criminality among adolescents with a cannabis use disorder. *International Journal of Offender Therapy and Comparative Criminology, 62*(6), 1573–1588. https://doi.org/10.1177/0306624X16687536

van der Pol, T. M., Hendriks, V., Rigter, H., Cohn, M. D., Doreleijers, T. A. H., van Domburgh, L., & Vermeiren, R. J. M. (2018). Multidimensional family therapy in adolescents with a cannabis use disorder: Long-term effects on delinquency in a randomized controlled trial. *Child and Adolescent Psychiatry and Mental Health, 12*, Article 44.

van der Pol, T. M., Hoeve, M., Noom, M. J., Stams, G., Doreleijers, T., van Domburgh, L., & Vermeiren, R. (2017). Research review: The effectiveness of multidimensional family therapy in treating adolescents with multiple behavior problems—A meta-analysis. *Journal of Child Psychology and Psychiatry, and Allied Disciplines, 58*(5), 532–545. https://doi.org/10.1111/jcpp.12685

VanderPyl, T. (2018). "I wanna make my mom proud of me": Embracing mothers as protective factors against future offending in delinquent youth. *Juvenile & Family Court Journal, 69*(3), 65–79. https://doi.org/10.1111/jfcj.12117

van der Stouwe, T., Asscher, J. J., Stams, G. J. J. M., Deković, M., & van der Laan, P. H. (2014). The effectiveness of multisystemic therapy (MST): A meta-analysis. *Clinical Psychology Review, 34*(6), 468–481. https://doi.org/10.1016/j.cpr.2014.06.006

van Vugt, E., Loeber, R., & Pardini, D. (2016). Why is young maternal age at first childbirth a risk factor for persistent delinquency in their male offspring? Examining the role of family and parenting factors. *Criminal Behaviour and Mental Health, 26*(5), 322–335. https://doi.org/10.1002/cbm.1959

Vardanian, M. M., Scavenius, C., Granski, M., & Chacko, A. (2020). An international examination of the effectiveness of functional family therapy (FFT) in a Danish community sample. *Journal of Marital and Family Therapy, 46*(2), 289–303. https://doi.org/10.1111/jmft.12405

Vermeulen, K. M., Jansen, D. E. M. C., Knorth, E. J., Buskens, E., & Reijneveld, S. A. (2017). Cost-effectiveness of multisystemic therapy versus usual treatment for young people with antisocial problems. *Criminal Behaviour and Mental Health, 27*(1), 89–102. https://doi.org/10.1002/cbm.1988

Vidal, S., Steeger, C. M., Caron, C., Lasher, L., & Connell, C. M. (2017). Placement and delinquency outcomes among system-involved youth referred to multisystemic therapy: A propensity score matching analysis. *Administration and Policy in Mental Health, 44*(6), 853–866. https://doi.org/10.1007/s10488-017-0797-y

Villalobos Agudelo, S. (2013). *The impact of family visitation on incarcerated youth's behavior and school performance: Findings from the Families as Partners Project*. https://www.njjn.org/uploads/digital-library/impact-of-family-visitation-on-incarcerated-youth-brief_VERA_April-2013.pdf

Visher, C. A., Debus-Sherrill, S. A., & Yahner, J. (2011). Employment after prison: A longitudinal study of former prisoners. *Justice Quarterly, 28*(5), 698–718. https://doi.org/10.1080/07418825.2010.535553

Vitopoulos, N. A., Peterson-Badali, M., Brown, S., & Skilling, T. A. (2019). The relationship between trauma, recidivism risk, and reoffending in male and female juvenile offenders. *Journal of Child & Adolescent Trauma, 12*(3), 351–364. https://doi.org/10.1007/s40653-018-0238-4

Voisin, D. R., Kim, D. H., Bassett, S. M., & Marotta, P. L. (2020). Pathways linking family stress to youth delinquency and substance use: Exploring the mediating roles of self-efficacy and future orientation. *Journal of Health Psychology, 25*(2), 139–151. https://doi.org/10.1177/1359105318763992

Wakefield, S., & Powell, K. (2016). Distinguishing petty offenders from serious criminals in the estimation of family life effects. *Annals of the American Academy of Political and Social Science, 665*(1), 195–212. https://doi.org/10.1177/0002716216633078

Walsh, F. (2012). Family resilience: Strengths forged through adversity. In F. Walsh (Ed.), *Normal family processes: Growing diversity and complexity* (4th ed., pp. 399–427). Guilford Press.

Ward, T. (2011). The Good Lives Model of offender rehabilitation: Basic assumptions, aetiological commitments and practice implications. In F. McNeill, P. Raynor, & C. Trotter (Eds.), *Offender supervision: New directions in theory, research, and practice* (pp. 41–64). Routledge.

Ward, T., Mann, R. E., & Gannon, T. A. (2007). The Good Lives Model of offender rehabilitation: Clinical implications. *Aggression and Violent Behavior, 12*(1), 87–107. https://doi.org/10.1016/j.avb.2006.03.004

Washington State Institute for Public Policy. (2019). *Benefit–cost results: Juvenile justice*. https://www.wsipp.wa.gov/BenefitCost/Pdf/1/WSIPP_BenefitCost_Juvenile-Justice

Weaver, B., & McNeill, F. (2015). Lifelines: Desistance, social relations, and reciprocity. *Criminal Justice and Behavior, 42*(1), 95–107. https://doi.org/10.1177/0093854814550031

Weisman, C. B., & Montgomery, P. (2019). Functional family therapy (FFT) for behavior disordered youth aged 10–18: An overview of reviews. *Research on Social Work Practice, 29*(3), 333–346. https://doi.org/10.1177/1049731518792309

Weiss, B., Han, S., Harris, V., Catron, T., Ngo, V. K., Caron, A., & Guth, C. (2013). An independent randomized clinical trial of multisystemic therapy with non-court-referred adolescents with serious conduct problems. *Journal of Consulting and Clinical Psychology, 81*(6), 1027–1039. https://doi.org/10.1037/a0033928

Weiss, B., Han, S. S., Tran, N. T., Gallop, R., & Ngo, V. K. (2015). Test of "facilitation" vs. "proximal process" moderator models for the effects of multisystemic therapy on adolescents with severe conduct problem. *Journal of Abnormal Child Psychology, 43*(5), 971–983. https://doi.org/10.1007/s10802-014-9952-z

Weissman, N., Batten, S. V., Rheem, K. D., Wiebe, S. A., Pasillas, R. M., Potts, W., Barone, M., Brown, C. H., & Dixon, L. B. (2018). The effectiveness of emotionally focused couples therapy with veterans with PTSD: A pilot study. *Journal of Couple & Relationship Therapy*, *17*(1), 25–41. https://doi.org/10.1080/15332691.2017.1285261

Welsh, B., & Greenwood, P. (2015). Making it happen: State progress in implementing evidence-based programs for delinquent youth. *Youth Violence and Juvenile Justice*, *13*(3), 243–257. https://doi.org/10.1177/1541204014541708

Westermark, P. K., Hansson, K., & Olsson, M. (2011). Multidimensional Treatment Foster Care (MTFC): Results from an independent replication. *Journal of Family Therapy*, *33*(1), 20–41. https://doi.org/10.1111/j.1467-6427.2010.00515.x

Whisman, M. A. (2019). Psychopathology and couple and family functioning. In B. H. Fiese, M. Celano, K. Deater-Deckard, E. N. Jouriles, & M. A. Whisman (Eds.), *APA handbook of contemporary family psychology: Vol. 2. Foundations, methods, and contemporary issues across the lifespan* (pp. 3–20). American Psychological Association. https://doi.org/10.1037/0000100-001

White, S. F., Frick, P. J., Lawing, K., & Bauer, D. (2013). Callous–unemotional traits and response to functional family therapy in adolescent offenders. *Behavioral Sciences & the Law*, *31*(2), 271–285. https://doi.org/10.1002/bsl.2041

Williams, L., Edwards, T. M., Patterson, J., & Chamow, L. (2011). *Essential assessment skills for couple and family therapists*. Guilford Press.

Wilson, H. W., Berent, E., Donenberg, G. R., Emerson, E. M., Rodriguez, E. M., & Sandesara, A. (2013). Trauma history and PTSD symptoms in juvenile offenders on probation. *Victims & Offenders*, *8*(4), 465–477. https://doi.org/10.1080/15564886.2013.835296

Wolff, K. T., Cuevas, C., Intravia, J., Baglivio, M. T., & Epps, N. (2018). The effects of neighborhood context on exposure to adverse childhood experiences (ACE) among adolescents involved in the juvenile justice system: Latent classes and contextual effects. *Journal of Youth and Adolescence*, *47*(11), 2279–2300. https://doi.org/10.1007/s10964-018-0887-5

Wolf Harlow, C. (2003, January). *Education and correctional populations*. U.S. Department of Justice, Office of Justice Programs, Bureau of Justice Statistics. https://www.bjs.gov/content/pub/pdf/ecp.pdf

World Health Organization. (2014). *Social determinants of mental health*. https://apps.who.int/iris/bitstream/handle/10665/112828/9789241506809_eng.pdf;jsessionid=F4D3D97CA5714422CD6E9A90DDB5E2B8?sequence=1

Wylie, L. E., & Rufino, K. A. (2018). The impact of victimization and mental health symptoms on recidivism for early system-involved juvenile offenders. *Law and Human Behavior*, *42*(6), 558–569. https://doi.org/10.1037/lhb0000311

Yoder, J. R., Brisson, D., & Lopez, A. (2016). Moving beyond fatherhood involvement: The association between father–child relationship quality and youth delinquency trajectories. *Family Relations*, *65*(3), 462–476. https://doi.org/10.1111/fare.12197

Youman, K., Drapalski, A., Stuewig, J., Bagley, K., & Tangney, J. (2010). Race differences in psychopathology and disparities in treatment seeking: Community and jail-based treatment seeking patterns. *Psychological Services, 7*(1), 11–26. https://doi.org/10.1037/a0017864

Zajac, K., Sheidow, A. J., & Davis, M. (2013). *Transition age youth with mental health challenges in the juvenile justice system.* https://www.umassmed.edu/contentassets/15113f8a672840fca8b783ca95a800af/taywithmentalhealthchallengesjj.pdf

Zeng, Z. (2019, April). *Jail inmates in 2017.* U.S. Department of Justice, Office of Justice Programs, Bureau of Justice Statistics. https://www.bjs.gov/content/pub/pdf/ji17.pdf

Index

R

S

T

U

V

W

Y

Z

About the Author and Series Editors

Corinne C. Datchi, PhD, ABPP, is an associate professor and chair of the Department of Psychology at William Paterson University. She is past president of the Society for Couple and Family Psychology, American Psychological Association (APA) Division 43. Dr. Datchi is also a fellow of Division 43 and a licensed psychologist with board certification in couple and family psychology. Her research and practice focus on correctional populations, reentry, problem-solving justice, and gender. She has written and published in peer-reviewed journals about family therapy, offender rehabilitation, and qualitative research methods. Her most recent contribution is a coedited volume published by APA in 2019: *Integrative Couple and Family Therapy: Treatment Models for Complex Clinical Issues*. Dr. Datchi is also the coeditor of *Gender, Psychology, and Justice: The Mental Health of Women and Girls in the Legal System*, published by New York University Press in 2017.

She is the series coeditor, with Dr. Anthony L. Chambers, of *Fundamentals of Clinical Practice With Couples and Families*.

Anthony L. Chambers, PhD, ABPP, is the chief academic officer at The Family Institute (TFI) at Northwestern University. Dr. Chambers is also the director of Northwestern University's Center for Applied Psychological and Family Studies and is a clinical professor in the Department of Psychology. He is a former president of the American Psychological Association's (APA's) Society for Couple and Family Psychology (Division 43) and a past-president of the American Academy of Couple and Family Psychology (ACFP). He currently serves on the Board of Directors for the APA.

Dr. Chambers received his BA in psychology from Hampton University and completed both his MA and PhD in clinical psychology at the University of

Virginia. He completed his internship and postdoctoral clinical residency at Harvard Medical School and Massachusetts General Hospital. Noteworthy academic achievements include coauthoring *Integrative Systemic Therapy* (IST), coediting the *Encyclopedia of Couple and Family Therapy*, and coediting a TFI book series on IST. Dr. Chambers's professional accomplishments have resulted in his becoming a fellow of the APA, a fellow of the ACFP, and a diplomat of the American Board of Couple and Family Psychology. He also serves on the editorial board of the journal *Family Process* and is the past associate editor for the journal *Couple and Family Psychology: Research and Practice*.